TOUGH ENOUGH

Lewis Tucker
Tough Enough

Published by BooxAi
ISBN: 978-965-578-484-8

TOUGH ENOUGH

(THE DIARIES OF THE TRANSFORMATION FROM CIVILIAN TO SOLDIER)

LEWIS TUCKER

CONTENTS

CHAPTER 1

HOW IT ALL STARTED

I must start by saying, I never intended to write this book. I only intended to document my journey as I enlisted in the armed forces.......... Ok, lies, lies (or, as the kids say nowadays, "Caps! Caps!"). I knew as soon as I enlisted, I was going to write this. As soon as I put the blunt down and realized I was signing up for the military, I knew I was going to write this book. Either it was some really good weed, or the military's marketing department is second to none because those commercials are hook, line, and sinker. I mean, they really make you feel like you can "Be all you can be," muthafuckin "Army Strong," "The Few the Proud," and all that shit. Uncle Sam will have you hook, line, and fucking sinker!

It was 2009, and I was 28 years old. I had moved back to Charlotte, NC a few years earlier from graduating college and still had no idea what the hell I wanted to do with myself. All I knew was what I didn't want to do and that was just be ordinary. Fall in line like all the others and just exist. Wake up, go to work, come home, eat, go to bed, wake up, and do it all over again. I had been doing that since I graduated from college and had never felt more unfulfilled in my life! I graduated with a degree in marketing and was working a job that had absolutely nothing to do with marketing. Zero! Zippo! Absolutely nada. As I sat thinking to myself, chilling with my partner DJ and maybe my Homeboy Kyle, I just remembered thinking, "There has to be more than this out there for me."

I remembered thinking and feeling slightly irritated that I had spent all my blood, sweat, and tears over a degree that, at the time, I felt was nothing more than an expensive certificate that got me a pat on the back and a good old fashion, "at a boy." I remember thinking I did all that work for my mother and grandparents to be proud of me and I didn't feel like I had accomplished a damn thing. You See, they raised me to think if I do well in school and I go to college, then I will have a good job and a great start in life. Those were the old days. In my eyes, in 2008 all I saw were bills, little food in the refrigerator, no woman on my arm, and my life not going the way I wanted or planned. Puffin on my Dutch Master cigar, drinking a beer, lying on my sofa, contemplating, and then what do you know? My sports center top plays get interrupted by an Army commercial. I mean, I was feeling Steward Scott delivering all of the high-flying highlights of the week, and then this commercial came on. "This is some bullshit..punk ass army commercial."

That's all I thought at first. Thought no more about it, hopped my happy ass up off the sofa to go grab another beer for me and my partner, went outside to check the mail, came back in and another fucking Army commercial came on. "Muthafucka, I can't get away from this shit," I thought. Yet this time, the commercial was action-packed. I mean it was muthafuckas swinging and droppin' down from choppas and shit, the wind blowing all camouflage out. I thought I was watching a movie for a moment. Then that's when it hit (all of it, the alcohol, the weed, and the big I dea). That was the moment everything changed. "I'm going to the muthafuckin Army," I told myself. I didn't put a lot of thought into it. I didn't contemplate for days or weeks about it. Enough was enough. I was tired of how I was living, I wanted more out of my life. I felt I had played my cards the right way, how I was told. I did good in school and graduated college. Never got in any serious trouble (no more than typical teenage boys do), but I didn't feel I was reaping any benefits of all that sacrificing I had done. I felt like I got screwed. I got the short end of the stick.

Why wasn't I able to travel and buy the nice things I wanted? Everything felt like Groundhog Day for me. Same old shit just a different day. I remember the feeling like it was 5 minutes ago, and I knew I wasn't going to put up with it anymore. "Aye yo… I'm going to the army," I announced to my pleasantly slumped over partners. I knew no one would believe me because for one, I was so anti-everything and two, I had a good head on my shoulders. For some stupid reason, people think, "Oh well, if you are smart, why would you go to the army?" I didn't care about any of that, and quite frankly, didn't even have time to entertain selling people on it being a good idea for me to go. I made a decision and stuck with my decision.

Shit was going to change from that day forward, and I was not changing my mind. Now, I didn't have all the answers, and I knew I didn't, so I did what I do best: research. I tried to look up any and everything I could find about what to expect when joining the armed forces. At no point was I scared, but more so curious. No one likes the unknown, so I wanted to prepare as much as possible. As I did my research, I found mostly information on what to expect from the physical aspect of military life and basic training. Push-ups, yelling, sit-ups, blah blah blah. Out of all the information available, I found truly little, if any information at all, on what to expect from a psychological standpoint.

I knew how to get my body right, but I mostly wanted to know how to get my mind right! What in the hell am I really getting myself into? That's what I wanted to know. So, being that I could not find enough information to satisfy my inquisition, I stopped looking. I was getting irritated and frustrated, as well as impatient, so I stopped researching. I said fuck it, I'll join and when I go, I'll write the shit myself. That's how this whole thing started. Anyone who tells you they joined the armed forces (especially the army or the marines) and nothing changed, or they stayed the same is a liar (they cappin', they cappin'). Now, I can't say I knew exactly how things would change, but I did know the change was coming.

CHAPTER 2

MAKING MOVES

I t's Final. Army, here I come. Only I wasn't just coming for shits and giggles like I was on some Bill and Ted's excellent adventure. I had a plan. You see, the way I was wired, I already had an attitude I was pissed things weren't going how I planned in life. Like I said, I felt I played the game how I was told it was to be played, only I felt like I was the one getting played. I still had a young mentality, thinking the world owed me a fucking favor. Real talk, on a miniscule level, I may have even felt entitled. I felt that because I put in the work of going to and graduating from college, everything else was supposed to just come, like the working part was over. I was full of resentment towards corporate America for not giving me an opportunity to make a name for myself in the field I had chosen to polish my skills. Therefore, I gave corporate America the proverbial "fuck you," and started the process of enlisting.

Before I enlisted, even though I came to the decision at a moment's notice, I took my sweet ass time figuring out exactly what I wanted to get out of my time serving. We all have had one of those "If I could do things differently, I would" moments. This time I got to capitalize on it. I always said I would have gotten a trade before going to college. This way, I would always have a skill to fall back on in the event I lost my position in corporate America. I wanted to save some money (at the time, I felt as if I was unable to do the things I wanted or felt I should be able to do). I also wanted to travel. I mean yeah, I had been to the beach, and I went to college away from my hometown, but the fact is I hadn't really experienced anything. I hadn't lived. I was existing. Going through the motion of carrying on with life, I wasn't living. I wanted to live and see how others lived.

For those who ask, "How do I enlist? Where do I start?" Start the obvious way with whatever branch you are thinking about and go to their website www.whateverbranch.com. Trust me, a recruiter will reach out to you probably before you even finish looking at the site. The military thrives off emotions, so they want to hook you while the feeling is still strong and the motivation level is high. Recruiters are salespersons, let's not forget, so numbers mean a lot to them. In my situation, I had a best friend (more like a brother) who served, and he just so happened to know a recruiter to connect me with. Typically, there are local recruiters in your city on your side of town in some middle-class strip mall or shopping center that would just love for you to swing their way. God's plan for us is funny sometimes, and we do not always know the details of the plan, but it seemed like all the stars were aligned for me to join the service. The recruiter just so happened to be renting one of our other best friends' childhood home, right around the corner from my house!

About a week after my friend introduced the two of us to each other, the recruiter and I met just for me to get a feel of what to expect. Now, these meetings are not formal sit-down meetings. They are more like kick it sessions (more like how you would court a love interest). He took me to eat, and we cruised around town, and I would just watch a day in the life of a recruiter. We went to the mall, downtown, high schools, and other recruits' houses. It was fun (like dates are supposed to be). I asked all the questions I could think of, but to be honest, you don't know what you don't know to ask. Recruiters make that shit seem like it's going to be as easy as pie. If they are any good at what they do, they will listen to you closely and paint the picture that you need to hear. Each recruiter's pitch is designed to make your life feel like it's going to be just what you dreamed. If you want to be a badass, they will paint the picture like you will no doubt about being a badass. Remember, the military feeds off emotions and capitalizes on feelings.

When you want to enlist in the armed forces and you are even remotely serious, outside of any felonies and serious physical concerns, recruiters will do everything they can to make sure you follow through with enlistment. They will help condition you physically, get clean to pass drug tests, and provide resources for legal issues that may need to be addressed, like child support, custody rights, property matters, you name it! Oh, you are the star of the show at that point! I met with my recruiter at least once a week until I left for basic training. I think part of it was to make sure that all was going according to plan, and the other part was to make sure I wasn't going to flake out and come up with some lame excuse at the last minute.

Once you are assigned a recruiter (usually the first recruiter to greet you at the door when you walk into the office), they schedule a date for you to take what's called the Armed Services Vocational Aptitude Battery test, also known as the (ASVAB) test. In short, the test determines which jobs offered in the branch of service you choose you would be most likely to excel in. Your recruiter will ask you what field you want to be in, but they would not really go into many specifics until after you test and the results are in. This way, your hopes do not get up in case you don't score high enough for your job field of choice. Word to the wise: You want to take the test seriously, just as you would the SAT, ACT, or any other test you deem important. When taking the test, remember it's not set up like a pass-or-fail exam. It's more like an assessment along the lines of a Wonderlic test, depending on what areas you do well in, depending on the opportunities and job selections available to you. Also, bonus money is attached to ASVAB scores along with Military Occupa-tional Specialties (MOS). If you don't know what you want to do, at least rule out what you know you don't want to do. This will save everyone time, and recruiters will have a better idea of what areas to focus on.

Everyone is different, and everyone has different reasons for enlisting in the military. To some, this may come as a surprise, but for most people who enlist, it is not to fulfill a civic or patri-otic duty. At some point, soldiers were civilians prior to enlisting too. Hell, people have bills to pay. Life can be a muthafucka. Parents were barely making enough to support kids, and kids were tired of their living conditions. Some people want a change in life, some think they have no other options, and some just simply are, well, running. The list goes on and on, but what you can pretty much bet on is they didn't join because they just simply love America. Sounds lovely, though.

CHAPTER 3
TEST DAY

T est day, test day! Being that I hate suspense and I wanted to get it over with, I took my test first thing that morning. I knew the test would take a few hours, so my recruiter told me it was possible to get my scores back the same day. The test started at 9:00 a.m., so my recruiter came to pick me up at 7:30 a.m. We went to eat breakfast somewhere, simple McDonald's or Burger King, some shit like that. As we ate, my recruiter asked if I was nervous. He couldn't have known that test taking was kind of my thing, so I stated boldly, "hell no." I guess that was his moment of relief because as soon as he realized I was serious, he chuckled a bit, devoured the rest of that McWhatever, gulped his last little swig of orange juice down and sat straight up. As I continued to enjoy my breakfast (being it was still early), My recruiter gave me the run-down of what to expect once we entered what's called MEPS (Military Entrance Processing Station) and how testing would go.

I wasn't worried about taking the test. I was more curious as to what jobs I would qualify for. As I said before, one of my objectives was to learn a trade, so I knew I didn't want to take a classification that would serve me no purpose once I got out. With that said, I also knew I wasn't trying to be Rambo or MR. G.I. Joe, none of that nonsense. I didn't have shit to prove to the point I needed to be that destructive. I was going through car issues at the time, and I always had a curiosity for mechanics and cars, so I decided once I found out my scores, I'd do something with mechanics. To me, that was practical and respectable. I knew that as a mechanic, you had to be smart and resilient.

As we pull into the parking lot of MEPS, of course, the first thing you see are recruiters, all in their various uniforms, all neat to the point of perfect (almost like they were trying to outdo each other), and then beside them, their recruits. Up until this point, I always thought I would be old going through basic training (and I was somewhat), but I saw people of all sexes and nationalities, but more so, I saw people of all ages, literally up until the cut off age of 42. Some were in shape, some looked focused, some looked confused, but they seemed like they wanted to be there.

The next thing I remembered was that everyone involved with MEPS was either active military or retired military. One facilitator said something to me that resonated immediately. As I Stood in line waiting to sign in, this tall, bold stature man came to the front of the line and stated in a loud voice, "The Military is a well-oiled machine! The one thing that keeps that machine running isn't rifles or missiles or bombs….. It's paperwork! The sooner you understand that, the better off you will be. Finish your forms, pay attention to what the fuck you are doing, and hurry up so you can wait!"

The wait wasn't terrible. As I sat there, I remember talking to a few recruits, swapping stories of what we thought was expected. Describing things we would love to do and places we would love to see, some of it was naive thinking I'll admit that. At this point, I was just killing time and making conversation. I also remembered, as I sat there amongst the different ranges of ages, how young 18 (in some kid's cases 17 if they have finished high school) really is. I was 29 and I thought, "Man, it's no way I could do this at 18."

As my name was called, I filed into the test room with the other recruits and was assigned a seat. Like most other testing locations, there was zero tolerance for cheating or falsifying documents, and each section was timed. I wasn't nervous, more anxious to get it over with. I didn't think the test overall was terribly hard. There were some sections here and there I did scratch my head on, but overall, it wasn't bad. Looking back on it now, I do wish I would have taken my time. So, for anyone about to take the ASVAB, take your time, and take it seriously!

I finished up the test confident I had done well, submitted my testing materials, and strolled out of the center. As I reached the lobby, I saw my recruiter sitting waiting anxiously like he was at Grey-Sloan Memorial waiting for Dr. Grey to deliver life altering news. As I approached closer and he saw me, he gathered his belongings, brushed his uniform off, and we headed off. "How do you think you did?" Those were the first words, of course. "It was cake," I replied. With a sigh of relief look on his face, he pointed to where he had parked the car, and we headed back to the recruiting office.

"Test results are in," one of the recruiters announced. Man, that was fast. I mean, I thought it felt like we took the long way back, kind of like we were stalling to get back, almost like a child stalls to get home if they know they are going to get a whipping. As my recruiter fumbled with typing and accessing my account, he started to explain a little more about what scores meant and how they could affect a recruit's negotiation leverage. Once he finally got into my account, he looked at the screen, looked back up at me, looked back down at the screen one more time, and as he looked up again, he had the biggest Kool-Aid smile on his face I had ever seen. "MY MAN!" he screamed proudly as if he had coached me up to achieve this magnificent score. He starts pulling out all these pamphlets and pictures and jobs and bonus structures attached to jobs. At this point, he was all over the place. Grabbing any and every piece of information, he had in his office to show me I could basically do whatever I wanted to do.

At this point, I started to feel a bit overwhelmed, so I decided to gather all the information and packets he had given me and review the information at home over the next few days to really see what I would have an interest in. Some jobs I had information on were practical, and some just sounded cool. Some came with great bonuses, but the job wasn't interesting, and some jobs sounded like perfect fits, yet the bonus pay was a little north of gas money.

I explained to the sergeant I needed to review by myself first, and once I had questions about anything I researched, I'd give him a ring, and we could go over things. I don't like to feel like I am being manipulated, nor do I like for someone else to decide my fate or persuade me into doing what they feel I should do. He understood (he had to because that's the way I said it was going to be) and said that was a wise thing to do. At that point, I proceeded with what I call the ol' "wrap em and dap em" technique. Wrap up the conversation, dap em up (that means shake their hand for you suburban folks) and get the hell on.

CHAPTER 4

CHOOSE AND CHOOSE WISELY

As I pondered on different jobs, I started to realize something important that I think most younger recruits may have noticed but may have downplayed. The more dangerous the job, the higher the bonus pay!

Damn. I ain't tryin' to get shot or blown up or none of that shit. I ain't that fucking hard, and shit didn't seem that fuckin cool or glamorous to me, at least not becoming disfigured. At the same time, I wasn't trying to be a pencil pusher either. I mean fuck, I wanna live, I wanted to have some stories to tell once I got out. That's what life's about. Isn't it? I knew I was done living in fear and in hopes of what others thought or wanted me to be. The cookie cutter mold wasn't getting it for me. I knew I wanted to do something respectable yet still macho enough not to get clowned by my partners at home. I damn sure was gonna be no fucking MP (military police). I already considered myself a damn good cook, so that was out of the question.

I came across this brochure for M1 Abrams tanks. Oh shit, this looks interesting. Then I saw another one. Bradley tanks, hmm, the fuck is this, I thought to myself. "Them shits look badass!" So, I read up a little about them, and then I asked my recruiter to give me the scoop on what he knew about the job. He told me you had to be smart to be a tank mechanic, and mechanics got respect. "Everyone respects mechanics," he stated. "You gonna be with the grunts, but hey, if shit hit the fan, who better to be with though, right," he asked rhetorically. He did have a point. Then to drive the point home, I was having car troubles at the time anyway. What better job to have, I thought. I'll be able to work on my own car."

That's the lightbulb that went off in my head. At that point, I knew mechanic it was for me I just had to decide what I wanted to work on. Not to go into job specifics too much, but I decided to work on Bradley vehicles because of the versatility. "Bradley mechanic, final answer," I said. My recruiter looked at me and nodded with a confirmation as if to say, "Yeah, bro, that's a good pick!" I kind of got the feeling he would have looked at me with a side eye if I said groundskeeper or some bullshit.

"Hey, battles!" he screamed. "We got us a 91 mike!" 91 mike is the job classification for Bradley mechanic. I asked if I would get to travel with that job classification, and my recruiter laughed. "Well, don't worry about traveling," he said. "While you're in the army, the one thing I guarantee you will do…is travel." Man, he never lied about that. I sat there for a few moments, just soaking in the idea that I was about to be a mechanic. "Ok, so what's the next step," I asked. I wanted to know everything right then and there.

Now here is where shit gets interesting. Most people think just cause you want to go to the army, you can just go. Wrong! Wrong, wrong, wrong. Yeah, Uncle Sam wants you, but I'll let you in on a secret: he doesn't like no bag ladies. All those court orders, tickets, and charges you thought you were going run away from? Nah, dog. His next step is clearing all that shit up. And oh yeah, the piss man, he wants you too! You smoke Tuck?" he asked. Fuck! "Smoke what?" I asked. He looked up from his computer with a little smirk on his face and said, "Mufucka, I ain't talking about no Paul Malls. Do you smoke weed? Do you blaze?" I paused for a second. Then as I was getting ready to say no, he said, "Cause if you piss hot, you can't go." Damn it. "Yeah, I smoke," I stated. "Gotdamnit! Well, how much?" he asked. Before I could answer, he just assumed I smoked every day, multiple times (and he was right) and told me he was going to give me a month to stop smoking and then pick a departure date.

I did it. I quit smoking. Right there on the spot, I knew I had a life changing decision to make. I could stop smoking and write a new chapter in my life and face some boyhood fears I had about growing up, or I could just keep living feeling entitled and getting nowhere. Fuck smoking when it came down to accomplishing goals. I had shit I wanted to do. Shit I needed to do. Not shit to do to prove something to anyone else. I had shit I needed to prove to myself as a man, as a young adult.

I waited a little longer than 30 days to let my recruiter know I was clean. I wanted to make sure that way when I took the test, and I wouldn't embarrass myself or my recruiter. Throughout the month of my detoxing, he would call or swing by the crib to check on me and make sure everything was all good. On the day I took my drug test, I knew we were going to look at leave dates. I also knew I wanted to leave as soon as possible, so I was ready to get it over with. It was getting late in the year and the last thing I wanted to do was go through basic training in the cold.

I arrived at the recruiting office early that next morning to take my drug test. I made sure to drink a lot of water the night before and that morning. My recruiter told me to pee first and then come to make sure what was coming out was clean water. I did just that and wouldn't you know it, I got the piss cup, and I didn't have to pee. It took me about an hour and a half to go again. My recruiter took the cup tested it, saw that the first test came back clean, and then we took the real test. After we got the results back from that test (which I also passed), he looked up some leave dates. I told him I wanted to leave as soon as I could. My birthday had just passed, and all my affairs were in order. He looked up at me once more from his computer with that grin of his and said, November 17th. The 17th was about two weeks away. I confirmed in my head the date locked it in my phone. I looked my Recruiter in the eye and said, "I guess the 17th it is then."

CHAPTER 5
LOOSE ENDS

amn, the 17th is like two fuckin' weeks from now. That's what I thought as I walked to my car, leaving the recruiting station. Fuck it, so be it then. All I knew was I was ready for change, and I was not waiting much longer for it either. I started going through my check list of things I needed to do and people I needed to talk to. At that time, I didn't really have too much value, so whatever I did have, I sold, gave away, or placed in storage in the care of two my most trusted loved ones Monica and Shakira. I knew they would take care of it as best they could (plus, guys will fuck your shit up; You ever want someone to take care of your shit, get a woman to do it).

I was already in the process of doing some home renovations, so luckily, there wasn't a lot of furniture in my house at the time when I was preparing to ship out. Instead of buying groceries and having to worry about throwing food out, I just ate up all I had left in the house. Asked a few neighborhood friends to keep an eye out on the spot for me and also let them know that my sister would be in and out of the house also.

What's funny is, as I was making my rounds of goodbyes, everyone was like, "Maaan, you ain't bullshittin', huh?" You really going?" Umm, yah, I'm out this bitch. I'm the type of person who believes you can put thought into decisions and don't have to take all year to make a move. I thought about it, decided it was a rational and even smart decision for me, and I stuck with my decision.

Now, with all this packing and giving things away, there was one last thing I forgot about. TYSON!! MY FUCKING DOG!! Fuck! What was I going to do? I totally forgot I had a dog. I had no idea what to do or who to give him to. No way in hell was I giving him to the pound, but I had no idea who would want a pit bull that I trusted would take good care of him. My friend Kyle told me about a guy around the corner from me that was good with dogs that wanted him. I went to meet the guy and check out the potential home for my partner in crime. Once I got a good vibe about the place, I gave the approval and let him know that he would become the proud new owner of a playful brindle pit bull. I hate I had to get rid of my dog. To this day, that's the only thing about the new chapter I had to start that I feel bad about. I didn't even want to say goodbye, so I dropped him off, and as soon as he started playing with the other dogs, I left. The only thing that made me feel better was that I knew he was in a home just as good as mine was for him.

Dropping the dog off my dog was the last thing I had to do. Now that that's taken care of. I was just kicking it for the rest of the day waiting for my homegirl Monica to get off work so she could take me to the hotel that night before shipping out. I had to be at the hotel by 6 or 7 p.m., so I did my last-minute checks and made sure I didn't leave anything out of my overnight. No sooner than I had put the lock on the back door, I got a call from Monica saying she was outside. I made sure to close the blinds, took one last look at my empty house and paused. At the time I remember thinking, next time I step foot back in this house, I'll be different. I didn't know how much or what would be different, I just knew things wouldn't be the same. I locked the front door, hopped in the car, and took one last look at the home I grew up in as we made a right at the stop sign off Kerry Lane.

CHAPTER 6
THE NIGHT BEFORE

1 1/17/09

I arrived at the hotel, and the first people I saw were, of course, recruiters outside the hotel dressed in their Class A uniforms (the formal wear like they wear at military balls and take pictures in). My recruiter couldn't drop me off due to some prior obligations, but it was cool. I didn't want a babysitter anyway. I gathered my things from the trunk of Monica's car and said my final goodbyes. Monica dropped me off, but Tramaine and Shakira also met me there to see me off. For a second, I almost didn't want to go once Monica started to cry. I hurried to shoo them off so I could focus on the new task at hand: adapting to a new way of life.

I stepped inside the hotel, bags in hand, with all sorts of emotions running through me. I was nervous, excited, motivated, determined, I mean, you name it. I felt like I was getting a new start, almost like I gave myself a second chance. Only this time, instead of feeling entitled, I felt grateful. Not necessarily grateful to the Army or Uncle Sam per se. More so grateful that God allowed me the thought processes to come up with a way to better myself and my situation. The almighty matched my want and my determination with an opportunity.

No sooner than I took four steps inside the revolving doors than I was greeted by a civilian worker who gave me a red ticket, reviewed my I.D., gave me two yellow tickets, a small itinerary, and a room key. She explained that the red ticket was a meal ticket for dinner, and the two yellow tickets were for two complimentary drinks from the bar as a token of appreciation for service. Already, I was starting to see some of the military perks. Immediately upon receiving my tickets, I saw some younger guys trying to bargain and trade meal tickets for drinks. "Damn kids," I thought as I headed to my room. But shit, I didn't blame them though. I was going to use mine, and it definitely wasn't a bad idea to scout out people who didn't drink to get their tickets.

We stayed at the Holiday Inn downtown Charlotte, which is a pretty comfortable hotel, and the staff was extremely thoughtful and gracious in extending all amenities to us. I scurried to my room to place my bags down so I could go grab a bite to eat. Being it was free and all. As I entered the room, I was greeted by a younger guy, whom I assume was in his early twenties, maybe 21 or 22, and he seemed so excited to see me. Maybe he was just excited to be getting away from home or some other unknown reasons, but nevertheless, he was excited. He did introduce himself, but I can't remember his name because that was the last time I saw the kid. I was coming in, and he was going out. I sat on my bed for a second and took a deep breath. "Ok, this is really it," I said aloud yet to myself.

I grabbed my room key and headed downstairs to the restaurant. The staff greeted me, took my meal card, and gave me a simplified menu to choose my meal from. It was basically a burger, a simple pasta dish like alfredo or spaghetti, grilled chicken with a vegetable side, and a piece of cake or pie for the dessert. As I sat waiting for my pasta dish, I took in the scene and absorbed the music from the live band playing on the stage to the left of me. Of course, I didn't know anyone yet, so I sat alone, but in the same breath, I never felt alone. The meal came out rather quickly (as expected with limited options and a large amount of people to feed in a certain amount of time), and it was enjoyable but nothing spectacular.

After I finished my meal, I decided to take a last mini stroll around a couple blocks downtown and smoke a Black and Mild before lying down for the night. I walked and called a few people to pass the time, then decided to head back. There was no wakeup call, and we were instructed to be downstairs in the lobby ready to go by 5 a.m. tonight (for the non-early birds). The last thing I wanted to do was be late or miss the bus. I said I wanted to be in bed by nine or so, and it was ten minutes till. I arrived back to the room and made sure all my belongings were still in order (in case I had to whoop some ass if my shit was missing). I watched a little bit of SportsCenter and dozed off.

CHAPTER 7
SHIPPING OUT

1 1/18/09

(Alarm sounds violently) I popped up abruptly. Damn, 4:30 a.m. came quick as shit! I fell like I just went to sleep. Excuse me, 3:30 a.m. is here! Breakfast was served from 4:00 a.m.- 4:30 a.m., so I had to scurry in a hurry to dress, wash my face, brush my teeth, and get all my shit together. I hurried downstairs to a nice serving of runny eggs, a somewhat dried out biscuit, and diced potatoes.

Sure enough, 5:10 a.m. came, and about six or seven Greyhound charter buses were lined up outside, waiting and ready to load up to depart for M.E.P.S. Once we arrived at the center, we retook the same screening test as prior. Wanting to make sure you were still telling the truth about never doing things like smoking weed (which I did), drinking excessive amounts of alcohol (which I did at times), and conducting a physical where you have to strip down to your underwear in a room with about 30 other guys. Once that's completed, the real waiting started. I woke up at 3:30 a.m., arrived at MEPS around 5:45 a.m., and was complete with my process by 10:00 a.m., but from that point, I was just waiting around for the next charter to leave Charlotte and headed for Fort Jackson. I was told it would be here in no time. Little did I know, no time meant 1:45 p.m.

Columbia, SC. Now, I was told about the epic wait at the in-processing center, so I was well prepared for that, but I had no idea that the wait I was in store for at the reception center would be ten times worse (I'll explain later).

We all fell in lines which were ordered alphabetically by last name. Medical records in hand, we all waited for our name to be called to board the bus. Standing by each bus was a drill sergeant verifying each person that was loaded on the bus by identification card and social security number. As we filed on to the bus, we were instructed to fill in from rear left to right.

Damn, I mean, they knew exactly what ass what to be in which seat. I sat down and watched the rest of the recruit's load on. As the last recruit stepped on the bus, the driver closed the doors, and a drill sergeant stood up in front.

"Mornin' everyone! I'm so excited you all could join us this morning. Really Quick before we roll out, I just want us to all kind of get to know each other. So, let's just start with introductions like name, where you're from and kinda go from there, ok?" Let's start with you, "What's your name, kid?" he asked. Then the kid, as he was told, starts to give his information, and I don't even remember the kid's name all I remember is, "I don't give a shit what your damn name is!! Do I look like I give a rat's ass what your damn name is, son? We ain't on no damn date, and don't try and hold my hand next! I got my eye on you!"

I, as we all did, sat straight the fuck up and was like, "Holy shit!" I mean, this muthafucka went in for like four seconds, and that got all our attention. He started screaming again, "The only damn name that matters from this point on until I say so is MINE. Not my real name, and it ain't no pansy-ass name like Jaimie or Shawn! For all you care, my momma named me DRILL SERGEANT. The last name doesn't matter cause you won't have that long to answer anyway. When I speak, you will reply and then end with a drill sergeant. "YES, DRILL SERGEANT! NO DRILL SERGEANT! THAT IS IT!" At this point, all I thought was not about home, or family, or friends. It was, "This muthafucka aint playin." I wasn't scared like the youngsters were, but I did rethink what the fuck I got myself into for a second. I was like, "Ok, here we go, Tuck." My head was in the game now.

I was locked in. I had a plan, I had goals, and I had a vision. I could see in a lot of the people's eyes they were scared, and it did almost feel like I was getting shipped off to prison (even though I've never been to prison and never plan to go). The fear of the unknown and unfamiliarity sets in. It's almost like the anxiousness that hits your stomach as you approach the peak of that first drop on a roller coaster. You know at that point there is no turning back. The big show is here now! As the drill sergeant sat back in his seat, the bus began to pull out. Then the kid next to me leans over to ask if I'm nervous. I looked at the kid for a second, then laid back and dozed off.

CHAPTER 8
WE HAVE ARRIVED

amn, that hour ride felt more like 5 minutes. My sleep was abruptly interrupted with a loud whistle blow that seemed to be coming from all directions, accompanied by a slightly intimidating shout, "WAKE UP, WAKE UP, WAKE UP, WAKE UP!" It was the damn bus driver. We were about a mile out from the Fort Jackson exit. At this point, we were instructed to get our identification cards out and hold them in the air. It almost felt like grade school. The security guards at the gates will be checking all identification cards prior to the bus entering the compound.

As the facility became visible and we approached the main gate, all the laughter and chatter that was heard throughout the charter bus came to a screeching halt. Like a "Ok, shit just got real" quiet. As the bus came to a stop and reality kicked in, we all frantically exited the bus to what was called the "reception" phase. Reception is what you civilians would call an orientation phase. Reception is a shocker. It's the strip down, shakedown, forget about everything you thought you were going to be process. No more commercials, no more cameras, and no more smiles and cheers. Reception (orientation) is a 4-day process of basic army dos and don'ts. You are officially becoming property of the United States of America Corporation. You get poked and stuck and pricked and pried on. Full physical inspections, vaccinations, medical history reviews, psychological evaluations, measurements taken, uniforms issued, and oh yes, HAIRCUTS!

Besides all the things to do we needed to scratch off our list, waiting around we would learn would be the worst. I mean, everything is a process. Let me break it down for you. The military works just like a machine, almost like a conveyor belt. We literally were fed through lines to be in-processed. There were so many people moving in all different directions, all trying to be processed and meet deadlines in order to hurry up to get to the next processing station to wait around in line again. Little did we know, soon as we stepped foot off that damn charter bus, training started. We were already training our patience. If you ever want to practice working on your patience, it's simple. Whatever you're doing in your daily routine, take the long way to do it, stand in the longest line, take the longest route, and take the road with the most stop lights. That's what it felt like we did. Army lines make the Department of Motor Vehicle lines look like the express lines in self-checkout. We are talking hours of waiting for 2 mins of work.

Now that you know what reception entails, let's get to it! As the Charter bus door opens and the hydraulic breaks come to a halt, drill sergeants pile on the bus, screaming for everyone to rush off the bus. We get off the bus and everywhere you look, there are nothing but drill sergeants. It seems everyone is a drill sergeant. As we got off the bus, we were told to grab two bags, it didn't matter whose bags, grab two and place them all in one line across the front and go get in the push-up position (or the front leaning rest position as the military calls it). I'm thinking, "Ok, this should be exciting. This should be fun!" I hurry and grab my two bags, place them nice and neat in the line, and then hurry to find my spot on the concrete slab and get in the push-up position.

As I lean horizontally, waiting for all to file off the bus and join the rest of us in position, I hear the groans and moans of the others all in push-up position. I'm thinking, "This ain't that bad." Then it felt like seconds turned to minutes, and those minutes felt like turned to hours by the time everyone got off the bus. After a few moments, I felt like a sumo wrestler was sitting on my back. Arms shaking, drill sergeants screaming to stop slump-ing. I figured by now everyone was in place and off the bus, and they were. So why are we still down here? Then one drill sergeant shouts aloud, "Nobody's knees are allowed to touch the ground. No one is given permission to sweat, and you better not call me Sir. I ain't no officer. I work for a living. When you answer any of us, you answer with a drill sergeant. Is that clear?"

We all got our welcome to the army speech lying in the starting push-up position. No greeting candy or card or balloon. No welcome soldier parades. Our welcome hurt; we were already windy and a little tired, and we hadn't even got our rooms yet. As a matter of fact, we hadn't done anything. We hadn't gotten up off the ground since we got off the bus, and that welcome speech was probably about 40 minutes long. I can't remember what was in it, all I remember is thinking, "When the hell can we get up?" My arms went from tingly to burning back to tingly, then just numb. After we got on our feet, we were given the task of figuring out whose bags were. This would have been simple enough, but we were only given five minutes for everyone to have their bag. If everyone didn't have their bag by the end of the five minutes, then we had to get back down in the front leaning rest position (not calling it push-up anymore, you should get the point by now) for two minutes and then try again. We repeated this process well, until we all figured it the fuck out and had our bags.

Now that everyone was off the bus, we all walked in 2 single file lines into a building that I believe was like a registrar's office. We were all instructed to pull out our MEPS packets and were given a beautiful welcome to Fort Jackson package that included all this stuff we wouldn't get to do and all these places we wouldn't get to go.

As we stood in our lines, most people were reading their packages or chatting quietly among themselves. I observed my surroundings. The first thing I noticed was there were no chairs. In all the rooms I was able to see, the only chairs I saw were behind the main desk in the front of each room. The rooms in the building I was in so far were set up like classrooms or learning environments. Pictures were hanging on walls, and state and national flags were everywhere, just no chairs.

We all had our packets, and from there were escorted to our living facilities. Oh yes, the barracks. This is the only thing

Hollywood gets right. Rows and rows of beds were lined up and aligned alike. All were uniformed, all dressed to the standard of perfection, just waiting for their next occupants. We were given five minutes to pick a bed, place our things down by our bunk, and return to the main entrance. There were no guided tours, no fresh minty chocolates on the pillows. In fact, there was none of that quite frankly because it didn't matter. It was time to go to work, and we were about to find out exactly what that meant.

CHAPTER 9
RECEPTION

Wakeup in reception was usually about 4:30 a.m. or 5:00 a.m. When it comes to the military and Uncle Sam, rule number one is: DON'T BE LATE! Please, if you take nothing else away from this book, understand this: don't be late, don't be late, don't be late! The best way to get labeled as a "shit bag" or bad soldier is to be late. It's the worst thing you can do. You will placed on all the shitty tasks, no one will want to fuck with you on a personal level, and it causes resentment. Just don't do it. With that being said, in the military, nothing is ever at the time it says it is. If you are told to report to formation at 05:00 military time (5:00 a.m. for you civilians), that really means you need to be there at about 4:45 a.m. to make sure you are accounted for and in place. 0500 means we are starting right at 5:00 a.m., not 04:59, not 05:01, right at 05:00. To be early is on time, to be on time is being late, and being late is unthinkable. If you get a 10-minute break, it's really about six or seven because you better be back by the end of 10 minutes, not on your way back, but back and ready to continue working or training. In this case for us, it was hurry up and get back to hurry up and wait.

In reception, wake up is at 05:00 for breakfast chow which is at 06:30, 06:45. Now I know whoever is reading this is like, "Damn, why such an early wake up?" The reason is that the chow hall (it's never called a cafeteria) literally has to feed an army. We're talking about 350-400, if not more, soldiers that all have to eat within an hour and a half. With that said, we were given 4 minutes to eat. That's 12 minutes a day: 4 minutes for breakfast, lunch, and dinner.

After breakfast, we were taken to the medical center, where we relinquished our medical records. We were taken to speak with doctors and psychologists for individual M.O.T.'s. Moments of truth where we are persuaded to reveal any medical issues that were withheld and any legal issues unaddressed that may be pending. The legal issues are any late-minute run-ins with law enforcement that may have happened after the military has already done its background check. After M.O.T.'s, we got shots. Now, the shots are a touchy subject, especially when it comes to your opinions on what's in them and if you believe what you are being told, but that is an entirely different subject. At this point, you are in the game, so you just must trust that you're being given what's being described. I will admit I was a little uneasy about it, but it is what it is. I will say this about the shots: they hurt! I felt like one shot went all the way to the bone in my arm!

On each day after we are done with shots, measurements, and medical evaluations, we get issued military apparel. Everything was issued in pairs. We got physical training (PT) uniforms first, which were nice windbreaker suits, training shorts (which were actually swim trunks), winter mock turtleneck t-shirts, summer t-shirts, winter beanies (skull caps or toboggans), black work gloves, green insert gloves for the work gloves, extreme cold weather gear which consisted of basically snowboarding gear. There was much more we got, like sleeping tents, camping gear, and so on. I can't even name it all, but you get the point by now. I felt like I was on some weird but very cool shopping spree. Each day we got different stuff, but the only thing they would not give us that we all wanted was the uniforms.

Man, I don't care what you say, you must admit military uniforms are clean! All of them: the formal uniforms (class A's) and the work uniforms (class C, better known as fatigues). I wanted the fatigues because I thought they were so clean and crisp. We didn't get those until the third day of reception. The reason being is that you can't just throw a uniform on. You have to be taught how to wear it. Can you imagine a bunch of civilians just throwing on all this different stuff and walking around? We would have looked like a hot mess. Not to mention, the Officers and Sergeant Majors (the big wigs) would have a fit. Once we got them and were taught how to wear them, we had an inspection to make sure everyone was dressed appropriately, or as we say in the military, "squared away." I will tell you now, and I'm sure my fellow comrades will agree, it was so worth the wait to get to put that uniform on. It was almost like a small rite of passage once we got them. The look of them, the feel of them, the sleekness of it all made you feel like a soldier. Still to this day, there's nothing like putting on a brand-new class C uniform, freshly ironed for the first time.

Day four was the final day of reception. By day four of reception, I was ready to get to my training unit. On this day, we got to meet our real drill sergeants. These are the badasses that will be training us and transforming us throughout the nine weeks of basic training. I was nervous, anxious, excited. I was ready. They came into our barrack late that morning after breakfast and shots. They didn't storm in screaming and cursing; they just gathered us around, introduced themselves, and gave us a little background on them and their resumes. We sat and talked with our drill sergeants for about 20 or 30 minutes and listened as they described what we were in for. As I looked around, I noticed everyone was soaking every word up. Now let me be clear, they were not being nice, so to speak, they just were not yelling, but I could tell these muthafuckas were not the ones to mess with. They all looked like they would fuck you up, and you believed it.

Once we were done talking, we were all instructed to gather all our things and head out to the front to meet the buses. At this point, I hurried up to grab my things, as we all did, and waited excitedly to load the bus. As we departed, I realized that we were just at a holding facility or campus. The actual base was huge! It took us about 15 minutes to get to the compound we would be staying at. As I gazed out the bus windows, All I could think was, "This place is huge!" As far as the eye could see was Fort Jackson. We saw other units running and training and grinding hard! Then it happened: we made a right turn headed towards these two story white buildings, almost like camp-style housing. Typical Barracks buildings like you see on TV. This time there were no flowers out front or any water fountains. There was a line of drill sergeants waiting for us and a big water tower with the words "Victory Starts Here," written on it.

The bus came to a slow halt, and the looks on the instructor's faces were stone cold! All of them looked ready to kill. Once the bus stopped, my heart sank, the nerves kicked in full throttle, and one kid behind me even vomited. A drill sergeant stormed on the bus and yelled, "EVERYBODY GET THE FUCK OFF MY BUS RIGHT NOW! MOVE! MOVE! MOVE!" That's when it happened. That was the day when all hell broke loose.

CHAPTER 10
WELCOME TO RED PHASE

1 1/22/2009

It would just happen to be my luck that my basic training would start on a cold, wet, rainy day. The steady drizzle of rain combined with the wind chill was not a good look. Not to mention, I think I'm getting sick. Today, we had this 8-hour class on ethics. It was damn near impossible for me to keep my head up and eyes open. My eyes felt like someone was holding a flame to them; they burned so bad from being so sleepy, and the 101-degree fever didn't help either. What really pissed me off was the punk-ass boys that slept in the bunks to the right of me. They kept the window open all night which I know fucked me up even more. I asked them to close it, but of course, they didn't. I don't want to start nothing though because I'll get kicked out for fucking up some little white boys.

Wake up tomorrow is at 04:00, so I am trying to prepare myself mentally for what's in store. I spent most of my free time this evening calling my loved ones and friends to let them know I made it safely. I love the support I'm getting from everyone, and I can tell I'm going to need it. When I spoke to my sister Lisa, I could tell she was concerned, so I didn't think it was the best time to tell her there was a possibility of me getting deployed to Afghanistan. But hell, I did enlist during a time of war, so she had to know that it was a strong possibility. Truth is, I don't care either way. See, before I enlisted, I did a lot of thinking about that and honestly, I felt like if it was my time to go, then it was nothing I was going to be able to do about it. But I know I'll be fine, I'm that dude! Specialist Tucker, look out world!

11/25/09

Damn, damn, damn. This is the first time I have had to write in like three days. Since the 22nd when I last wrote, a lot has gone on! Let me start by saying this (long sigh), soon as we got off the bus, we got our asses handed to us on a platinum platter. Once again, when we got off the bus, we were told to line our bags up in specific orders, and of course, it took the longest to complete such a simple task. Well, at least I thought it was simple. Since we couldn't get it right, we got our first Army lesson. Lesson number one: pay attention.

The way the army teaches lessons is by what is called holding "smoke" sessions. If you're thinking like I thought, no, this isn't that type of smoke session. No weed getting rolled up here. No sir, you see, this here is some serious conditioning. So serious, by the time you finish, you will be able to see the steam coming from your head (hence the term smoke). In this particular smoke session, we did 150 push-ups. Now, I know some of you are thinking, "Ok, that's not too bad." Think again. This wasn't just you getting down and doing 150 what you call push-ups, we had to pause in the down or up position (whenever we were told to stop pushing) and scream out, "Need more Discipline!" drill sergeant cursing our cold, wet asses out while we are eating mud, all over how we lined the bags up! Immediately, I knew this was going to be the longest, toughest 10-12 weeks of my life.

11/23/09 (recap)

Lights out (bedtime) was usually around 9:30 p.m. or 21:30 military time. The only difference now was that during night hours in the barracks, we had what is called fire guard duty. Fire guard duty is keeping watch, being security to make sure everyone is safe, and in this case, the barracks were secure. Guard duty is one hour rotating shifts, and my bunkmate and I had second watch tonight. Now, it just so happened that my bunkmate was assigned to be my battle buddy. A battle buddy is basically your twin; you go nowhere without them, and you are responsible and accountable for each other. So far, it's been working pretty good, but we were just starting, so we shall see.

11/24/09 (recap)

Moving on, so the second day, wake up was at 05:00, and formation was at 05:30. Once the clock struck 05:30 and everyone wasn't there, everyone that was there immediately got smoked until the formation was complete. Once everyone was there, we formed up, saluted the flag, and proceeded to get smoked again for not being on time. Push-ups, sit-ups, jumping jacks, front leaning rest position. It felt like it would never end. All the while getting cursed out about how selfish we were. Cried out about how undisciplined we were. And I have to admit, we were undisciplined. "Need more…Discipline!" we all continued to scream as we got dumped on by the rain and smacked in the face by the stinging wind. Some say look at it like a work-out. Hear me and hear me good, Fuck…That..Shit!! Work-outs are 45 minutes, maybe an hour. Nah, this shit was indefinite. Sporadically shit could just pop off, something could trigger a sergeant, and now we are at it. Pushing the earth down, as we say. Until drill sergeants were done venting, it would continue, and drill sergeants have huge egos. They love to talk and brag about how badass they are. So needless to say, we made the ground our home.

Today we had all classes. I hate going to classes. Not because I don't like to learn. I love learning, and it was the sitting I hated. Remember when I told you the only chairs I saw were behind desks in the rooms? That's because those are the only chairs allowed. We had to sit on hard ass tile floors Indian style. I hadn't sat Indian style since the 2nd grade. I didn't even know if I could still sit Indian style. To make it worse, the classes were in trailers. Can you believe this shit? There are probably about 50-60 fuckin soldiers packed in a trailer, sitting Indian style for an hour and a half interval. For me, it was torture, so I stood up against the wall in the back. It wasn't ideal, but hell, at least I had the wall to lean on and it was better than having my ass hurt for the next 30 minutes after we got up from sitting on that hard ass floor.

Lunch Is served promptly at noon every day. We don't get to eat lunch at noon every day or any day so far. Why, you ask? It's because we have females in my basic training platoon. This is very important for you fellas out there, so check it out. Co-ed basic training is a muthafucka. Females (some, I'll even say most) will fuck your shit up! Females will have you getting smoked all the time. Females want to make sure hair is done, females don't want to get down in the mud, females don't want to follow dress codes, females don't like bugs, but worst of all, females don't care about time, at least not before looking presentable. God forbid a war breaks out and the females don't have their freaking hair together! All I could think was, this is going to be a long ass 10-12 weeks.

You would think that getting "smoked" is something that you would get used to. Hell, no! You don't get used to it physically or mentally, but over time, you do learn to deal with it. I said fuck it, I ain't gone "deal" with it, I'm going to enjoy that shit. I mean, what else do I have to do? Mentally, you have to take yourself to another place, another comfort zone, because once the smoking starts, it's not stopping for a while. Now, there is an art to getting smoked, and most, if not all, drill sergeants are very creative with their element of surprise when it comes to springing a good ol' smoke session on some "green" soldiers. I learned quick, regardless of what a drill sergeant says, if you hear the command "half right, face," just know you are about to get smoked! If you ask a question or someone asks a question that has already been addressed, we got smoked. If anyone sighs or huffs and puffs about a task, we get smoked, pretty much anything other than "Sir, yes sir," you can bet there was a smoking involved.

Originally, at M.E.P.S. and during reception, we were told that drill sergeants are there for guidance and to help with your development, BULLSHIT! You are your own motivation. You will get told a lot by drill sergeants that basic training is all a game, and it is. The physical game is to get your body used to being uncomfortable and in uncomfortable situations. The physical game is also to get you accustomed to lugging around heavy equipment and functioning in heavy gear or what's known as a "full battle rattle." It's funny I write all this about it being a game, but as I lie here, my arms, chest, stomach, and legs tell me otherwise. I must admit, there were times during today that I did second guess my decision. I just chalk it up to all the smoking we were getting tormented with.

CHAPTER 11

SMELLS LIKE TEAM SPIRIT

1 1/25/09

As for today, the third day of basic training, it was fun as hell! Today, for the first time since I left home, I wasn't either tired, cranky, or displeased in the slightest. I think it may have been the long-drawn-out prayer I had last night (thank you, God, for hearing me). I prayed for all kinds of things I needed to keep me going like I was a kid on Christmas Eve. I only kept thinking, "If I could just get every day to be like today, I'll be just fine." Not to mention, today is Thanksgiving. Well, today is the day before, but it was the day we were celebrating Thanksgiving because the chow hall will be closed tomorrow. Everyone was so excited about Turkey Day! I thought it was a setup. I mean, I know how much these drill sergeants liked smoking us, and they kept telling us all the different things that would be served and how there was no need to ask us what we ate because they would see it later. Every time they mentioned how they would see it, everyone laughed. Everyone but me, that is, because I knew they meant it. We shall revisit this in a second.

We did have class today, and I actually enjoyed it. Some type of Middle Eastern culture class. The class was led by two soldiers who taught us a few words (I can't remember the language) and basically gave us a briefing about ways of the land and some other dos and don'ts if we ever get deployed to these areas. It was more like a "don't do this, don't do that, or shit could get you killed" type of thing.

I thought about My sister Lisa today. I think I was more concerned about how she was doing versus how I was holding up. This was my only blood sibling, and we weren't close growing up, even though we were raised together. My family is small, so it was just me and my sister left. Even though we weren't the closest, I still loved her and wanted to make sure she knew I was ok. I figured I'd call her as soon as I could, although I wasn't exactly sure when that would be.

Oh, before I forget, I can't believe I almost forgot the absolute best part of the day. Today, we were issued our official military M16 assault rifles. Getting issued your rifle is just like meeting your first love for the first time. We were all nervous, excited, anxious. I mean, you name the feeling and that was all of us. Giddy, like little schoolgirls. We all waited in line, talking about how we couldn't wait to "fuck some shit up" and how we were ready to go. Troops all fired up, and not one person fired one round yet. We didn't even know how to load the ammunition yet we were ready for war (laughs). I chatted with fellow battle buddies, and in a way, it was all funny, but in the same breath, as I glanced around, I saw this was the first time we didn't see each other as strangers. This was our first bonding experience that I recognized. Even though we were only in the first week, still, I felt damn near like a month, and we had gone through a little bit to share and talk about, at least what we thought was something.

As the drill sergeants gave us a small briefing on how things would go, the soldiers who ran the armory opened the gates, and we single-filed through the line. Now, this wasn't just a "Hey, go grab you a rifle and come back." No, no, no, in no way is this how that works. They have that shit on lockdown. It was soldiers and drill sergeants holding rifles to scare us to make sure no one tried anything stupid like, of course, stealing. These weapons had serial numbers, platoon numbers, company numbers, log out sheets, and ID numbers. If anyone took anything or lost anything, they knew exactly who it was.

Now let me break this down to you as far as weapon assignment cause this shit is important and can save your life! All that shit you see on TV about shoot-outs and bang-bang scenarios, that shit is all Hollywood! People running in, guns waving every-where, and people loading the chamber every five seconds. That shit just looks good and sounds good for television. Anyway, as we filed in, we were handed two M16 magazines, a red muzzle safety for the barrel of the rifle (safety precautions), a carrying strap, a cleaning kit, and your M16 rifle. Aw man, was she sexy!

As we were handed our weapons, we were instructed to hold our weapon with the barrel always facing the ground and to never place our finger on the trigger unless instructed. We were also told that at any point our finger is caught on the trigger uninstructed, that would be taken as an act of aggression, and we would be detained and pretty much get the shit kicked out of us. Considering what was at risk, I could understand this stance.

As we exited the arms room, we were instructed to return to the front of the barracks and form up out front. This was big for us because this signified the next step in basic training. We didn't look like civilians anymore, we didn't dress like civilians anymore, and now we had the most official thing that solidified our transformation: our rifle. "Never call it a gun, gangsters and thugs carry guns or waive guns," as we were told. Your rifle is an extension of you in the military. It's not an accessory. It's not something you grab heading out the door like a hat or umbrella. Your rifle is like a third arm or leg. You eat, sleep, shit, run, study, train, and go through everything there is to go through with your rifle attached to you. The only thing you can do without it is take a shower, literally. If you really want to experience pain and the closest thing to hell you can imagine…..leave your rifle somewhere. If you want to commit suicide, lose your rifle.

In the event of a misplaced weapon, the company goes on lockdown until the weapon is recovered. During lockdown, the entire company is looking for the weapon. The platoon that the soldier belonged to that lost the weapon will get all of the shitty details (details are work assignments handed down by the sergeant major that need to get done). The platoon is getting smoked until the rifle is recovered, and the soldier – well, the soldier is embarrassed. The soldier is placed on everyone's shit list for being the reason we got smoked, and now the soldier may be labeled a shit bird or bad soldier depending on how well they have been excelling in other areas, especially PT (physical training).

Today was a lot, so off to bed it is for me for now. Fireguard duty awaits, and I can't remember what time our shift is. It wouldn't be so bad if it was at the end or the beginning of a shift. But when you have it in the middle of the night or a few hours prior to wake-up call, just be prepared to operate tired that next day. Hell, I guess it doesn't matter anyway because we all are tired even if we do get continuous sleep. The change in environment and just the way you knew life in general is all different now, and that itself takes time to adjust. The only difference is, in the military and basic training, time is the one thing you do not have the luxury of wasting.

11/26/09

Today is officially Thanksgiving, and it was full of surprises. Oddly enough to say, shockingly, they were all good surprises. For you to get the full effect, let me start with last night. Last night I slept like a freaking baby. Now, let's not get it twisted: it wasn't a full 8 hours of sleep (who gets 8 hours of sleeping in basic training?), but it was noticeable rest. As 05:00 rolled around, I was already up and alert, just waiting for the wake-up call. I leaped out of bed at the sound of the doors being swung open by the drill sergeants. I was the first to finish dressing, shaving, and being ready to go out front prepared for what the day may bring. Mentally, I felt really good.

As I was securing my locker and about to head out to formation, BANG! The door flew open, and of course, here comes a drill sergeant, "What the fuck are you guys doing still in the gotdamn bay? The entire platoon is out front waiting on you!" Just as he was about to open the door to exit, he noticed the trash can was still full from yesterday. Apparently, the assholes who had the last shift of fireguard didn't take out the damn trash. "Muthafucka," I thought to myself. At that point, I knew what time it was. Then the drill says it, the words we all hate to hear but knew were coming. "Assume the position, move," he yelled. Of course, what better way to start the day off than by getting smoked? Here we are 05:00, pushing. We haven't even stepped foot outside yet, and here we are getting smoked like Jimmy Dean's finest.

While we were getting our asses handed to us, another drill sergeant walked in, heard what was going on, and decided to join in like we weren't getting sufficient punishment. This drill sergeant starts throwing everything on the floor. Dumping trash everywhere, knocking shit over, just going crazy. Then they announce we have 30 seconds to get to formation. We all stormed out of the barracks to make it to the formation, only to find the rest of the platoon getting smoked, waiting for us to get there. Once we arrived, we all got smoked together. Now, this is two smoke sessions we have had, and it's not even 06:00, nor have we done PT yet. PT always starts the day off, and today was cold as hell.

So, we go through the normal routine of classes and marching sessions. We march everywhere to learn rhythms and cadences. Marching keeps everyone uniformed. Everything in the military is about uniformity, as they say. As the morning approached about 10:45, we headed back to the barracks for a team meeting. Let me tell you, this "team meeting" started out the first 15 minutes of a meeting, then it turned into an hour and a half smoke session. I swear that's all the drill sergeants live for. By this point in training, I didn't even get mad anymore. Hell, some of the sessions I started to enjoy.

This is when, psychologically, you must find another place to go. Take your mind off all the negative things going on around you, take your mind off the fact that family is not around, off the fact that none of this is comfortable, and definitely, off the fact that we still have months to go of this bullshit. At some point, unde-nounced to me, the smoking actually became liberating. Through the mist of all the push-ups and sit-ups and wall sits, and flutter kicks, and any other various forms of exercise, the drill sergeants did explain the purpose of it all, and even though we didn't all know it, things were starting to sink in. I think this was a pivotal point in training, and there was a consensus with both our drill sergeants and the platoon.

For the remainder of the day, we watch this HBO special called Band of Brothers (Army shit, of course). A lot of soldiers were all rowed up, but honestly, I didn't see what the big deal was. Bunch of white boys I personally couldn't relate to, but if they liked it, I loved it, anything was better than getting smoked again, so Band of Brothers it was.

CHAPTER 12
LET THE GOOD TIMES ROLL

1 1/27/09

Today was fun as hell. We started learning the fundamentals of hand-to-hand combat today. Just so happens that my platoon drill sergeant is an expert in hand-to-hand combat. We, of course, had our safety briefing about how you may get hurt but suck it up blah blah this builds character, shows heart, and all that "rally the troops" shit. Now don't get me wrong, all of the rallying does work. We first started with some basic defensive moves, then moved to bayonet training, and then defensive moves and counter moves. From hand-to-hand combatives, we moved on to what's called pugal sticks. I've known them as joust sticks (the big ass Q-tip sticks) they used in the show American Gladiator). We had to wear protective gear, of course, but who cares? We still got to kick the shit out of people. I think I just may be starting to get the hang of this basic training thing.

I've started to recognize frustration triggers, I've learned to suck up the smoke sessions, and as a team, we are starting to trust each other. Not saying I think it's starting to get easier by no means. I just understand why we go through what we go through. I understand why the drill instructors have to be no-nonsense leaders. These are life and death scenarios they are trying to get us accustomed to so that nothing is unfamiliar territory. Recognizing scenarios is essential to psychological health and strengthening. Once you are able to recognize the scenario and understand what the lesson is, mentally you can embrace it and comprehend that the physical work is to strengthen your body, but it also strengthens your mind. Uncomfortable scenarios allow you to put your confidence on display. These scenarios help you face fears and show you characteristics about yourself you may not have known about.

During one of our mid-day marching sessions, we started learning these three chants (call and response tools for motivation) that I must admit sound quite disturbing. I guess the army says you can't be too nice when you training people how to kill. Nevertheless, it was all exciting, and it did make me want to stab the shit out of something also. The first call and response went something like this:

Drill sergeant: "What do we do?"

Soldiers: "Kill, kill, kill with no mercy, Drill Sergeant!"

The second call was:

Drill Sergeant: "Why did God make the sky blue?"

Soldier: "Because God loves the infantry!"

(I don't understand this one, but whatever).

The third call was:

Drill Sergeant: "What makes the grass grow green?"

Soldiers: "The blood, the blood, the bright red blood Drill Sergeant!"

That's horrible! You mean to tell me all this time I been fertilizing my yard and what I really needed all the while was some blood? Who knew? Ha ha ha. All combative order responses are "kill."

Once we were done with hand-to-hand combative training, we learned how to crush a person's skull with the butt-stock of our rifle. Then we learned how to disembowel an enemy with the bayonet. I mean, I felt like fucking Rambo or the damn Terminator for a while. I know I'm not the most hard-core person to walk the streets, but where I'm from on the east side of Charlotte, you can't teach any of those guys this kind of stuff. Bad idea. Crime rates will skyrocket. I mean, we are learning how to properly fuck shit up, how to thoroughly demolish an opponent. Street guys are the wrong people to try to teach this stuff to. No wonder we had so many psych evaluations and character questions.

Once combative training was complete, we had classroom training for the remainder of the day and finished it off with a question-and-answer session with Drill Sergeant Branch (she was one of my favorite instructors, a no-nonsense type woman but very fair. If she smoked you, you knew you deserved it, and no one, I mean no one questioned her. Very well respected and well deserved). She told us one thing today that I will never forget (I'll explain in a minute). While we were waiting for the drill sergeant to come in, this one girl wanted to open her big mouth and always acted like she was in charge, always wanting to command and order people. This one guy cursed her out, so since she couldn't take the heat, she wanted to tell the drill instructor once she arrived, and we all got smoked for her stupidity and pettiness (including her).

Once we finished pushing and doing some jumping jacks for about 10 minutes, we were all instructed to have a seat or "grab some tile." One female soldier started to snicker during the session while talking to another battle buddy, and Sergeant Branch called on the young lady to ask what the snickering was about. The young lady raised her hand and asked a question I thought was going to get us all killed. "Drill sergeant, a few of us wanted to know why you are so mean? Some people think you can act like a real bitch sometimes."

We all turned towards the young lady with a look of disgust and anger in our eyes. I just knew we were all getting smoked until midnight for that question. Then Sergeant Branch stood up from her chair really calmly which scared the hell out of me and said the most profound thing I ever heard. It wasn't really directed towards the men, but we definitely needed to hear it. Sergeant said, "Let me tell you something and you hear me good when I say this. There are two types of women in the Army, bitches and hoes." She paused for a second, walked over to the young lady, and said, "And I'll damn sure be that BITCH, before I become that HOE!" How can you argue with that? Once she said that, we all just got up, stood at attention, commanded our own half right face, and got down and smoked ourselves. Out of respect for her, we did that. From that day forward, we jumped at every command she gave before she could even finish giving it. I'll always remember that moment and I'll always remember that statement. I hope every woman teaches her daughter that philosophy.

All in all (in my Ice Cube voice), I have to say that today was a good day. Tomorrow is officially the last day of the first week of basic training. Come on, Christmas break! Even though I haven't been gone that long, I miss my family and friends. Even though my sister and I are not extremely close, she is my blood, and I do love her. My real support comes from my sisters from another mother. Lying in bed at night trying to fall asleep gives you time to think about a lot of things. It's funny the things and people you take for granted when they are easily accessible. Okay, signing off, who knows what tomorrow will bring.

11/28/09

Well, another day down and another day that was fun as hell. We started learning how to actually handle and break down our assault rifles. We also reviewed some hand-to-hand combat skills. We started to really get into how to fuck a mutherfucker up. I was so engulfed in the art of combat. I soaked up every word. I thought it was fascinating learning how to choke someone out in a few seconds in different positions. We were taught how to escape choke holds, and we learned how to break arms and tear tendons and muscle tissue in the process. You couldn't tell me I wasn't Bruce Lee or at least Bruce Leroy out this bitch. When I get to my duty station, I have got to take more combative training. That shit is way hardcore.

So, at this point, I think I have mastered the art of getting smoked. Physically, it still was tough, but mentally, it was nothing to me anymore. I think I was to the point I could get smoked all day and not care one bit. Now, I wasn't quite ready to put that theory to the test, but if it came down to it, I'd be like, "Let's do this." The only thing that gets to me is this one dumb ass drill sergeant that keeps taking our food trays too early. I think he gets a hard on by doing that. I mean, come on, we only get fuckin four minutes to eat as it is anyway.

Being in basic training, there are only a few things you have to look forward to throughout the day: mealtime, personal time, and bedtime. Don't deprive me of my mealtime, for heaven's sake. When the drill instructor pulled that bullshit today, I was like, "You gotta be kidding me?" I was right in the middle of my macaroni salad. If you don't know me, know this: There are three things in this world that I love: a nice woman, weed, and macaroni. I felt violated, like I had just been felt up or something. He pissed me off to the point I thought it was going to ruin my entire day. I didn't let it, though. I just remembered why I'm here, and I am going to complete the job I came here to do.

Tomorrow is Sunday, and my goal is to go to church, something I haven't done in a long time. This may sound bad, but I was going to make it a point to go to Sunday service. I just found out that's the only place drill sergeants won't be. I finally got a chance to write, so I wrote my first two letters since I arrived at Fort Jackson. I'll try and write more tomorrow if time permits.

11/29/09

Today was another good day. Today was actually pretty chill. We were awakened for an early chow, and today we actually got more than 4 minutes to eat each meal (not much more like 7 minutes or so). But by now, a seven or eight-minute time span feels like 30 minutes to eat. We stayed in the bunks all morning, and the only task we were given was to clean the bunks and make beds until lunchtime. The only thing that sucked about this was we were not allowed to go to sleep. After lunch, we were given some bullshit half ass jobs to do lick, go outside and pick rocks out of the sandpit (the beach as we call it), vacuum the classroom floors, bullshit, bullshit, bullshit.

We have this event tomorrow we are supposed to do at Victory Tower. Everyone's so excited about it, and it's supposed to be a big deal. Victory Tower is basically this big ass 30 or 40 foot wall we have to scale and propel down the other side. I'm definitely excited. My only reservation is it's supposed to rain tomorrow. Of course, weather means nothing in the army. That just means it gives drill sergeants an excuse to have us break out our ponchos or some other wet weather gear to try out and call it a day. Ok, that's It for today. I have fireguard duty at like 02:00. Tomorrow's journal entry should be interesting. Hope I don't break a leg or anything.

11/30/09

Wow, I can't believe tomorrow is the first of December. We get to go home in 16 days! That's awesome! Just like today was freakin' awesome! I mean, from wake-up until this very moment, today has been great. We did go to Victory Tower today, and that was an experience I will never forget. I am so glad that I didn't miss it either. This experience is one of those experiences you sign up for the military to have. It's one of those army commercial scene type of events. Ok, let's be back up a minute and start over from the beginning. Breakfast was like freaking 15 minutes long, and I got stuffed. By now, I didn't even need the entire 15 minutes to eat, and I was able to eat everything. That NEVER happens. I'm talking pancakes with fruit topping, biscuits, grits, eggs, and orange juice. I didn't know what to do with myself.

After breakfast, we formed up and marched back to the barrack where we met the rest of the company to road march to victory tower. Victory Tower is an elaborate 4-part obstacle course designed to build confidence and strengthen team building and bonding. There is a 40-foot-high hang net you have to scale and repel. There is a 40-foot-long rope hanging about 50 feet in the air, we had to crawl across, and then there is the actual victory tower. Victory Tower itself stands about 65 feet in the air, so there is a latter you have to climb up the tower. The first part of the ladder is a board and rope; the second part is an actual ladder you climb, and then you propel down the other side with a rope. I felt like an 8-year-old at recess. I'd never done anything like that in my life. It was exhilarating. My adrenaline was pumping something fierce, what a great rush! I did get smoked by some drill sergeant I didn't know for talking in line, but fuck it, I didn't care. It was worth the hype, and I would do it again.

For lunch, we dined on the ever so delicious meals ready to eat (MRE). I got one of my favorites, cheese tortellini with cinnamon apples. In the military, you start to appreciate the simple things in life. After lunch, we marched back to the barracks and stayed there until dinner chow. I was able to write a few more letters to friends back home, whom, by this time I had missed dearly already. There really wasn't much assigned to us except cleaning gear and turning in equipment from the march.

Oh shit, a crazy but funny as fuck situation happened today at dinner. Everything was going as normal. We all filed in the cafeteria as usual, got our food, sat down, and ate. As time was winding down, we had this one drill sergeant who didn't like mealtime anyway, so he always gave us the shortest amount of time to eat. He yells out, "Ok, you all know the deal, stack that shit." "Stack 'em," means right then and there, put your fork down, put your cup down, don't digest shit else, don't swallow shit else. As a matter of fact, whatever is in your mouth when "stack em," is yelled out, you better spit that shit out too. Pass your trey to the left and get ready to line up and leave.

Out of the corner of my eye, I see these two females still trying to hurry and sneak in a few extra gulps of their drinks. No sooner than I see this, I hear the drill instructor scream, "Hey you, two geniuses, stop fucking drinking and stand the fuck up right fucking now!" I'm thinking, "Oh shit, what the hell is this crazy muthafucka about to do?" I'm telling you; you never know with these drill sergeants' man. They get really creative when it comes to torturing us. Even more so than what is he about to do, I'm thinking what is he about to make them do? He scrambles over to the two female soldiers frantically and says, "So, you ladies still thirsty, huh?" No one says a word. "I asked a question," he stated. "Ok, ok, I get it. It was a long day. You want more to drink, I understand, and I apologize. Pull out your canteens." The two ladies looked at each other, confused like he was speaking a foreign language or something. "I SAID PULL YOUR GOTDAMN CANTEENS OUT AND GET EM OUT RIGHT FUCKING NOW AND HOLD THEM HIGH IN THE AIR!" It's on now. At this point, it's a show, so everyone in the cafeteria is looking at the scene. "Now drink water until your 2 quarts are empty, and then turn the canteen upside down over your head so I can see." Damn, this muthafucka is the truth is all I was thinking. I thought it was genius. I never would have thought to do that. Immediately, both the females started to bawl, crying.

We all stood there trying our best not to burst out laughing as the females cried and drank water. Water was running down both their faces; it was hysterical. Once both females emptied their canteens, they held them upside down over their heads, and the drill sergeant made them refill them and drink them all again as he lectured a hole in our heads about how when he says something, he means it and we don't know shit blah blah. Honestly, I heard nothing. I couldn't get over the look on these females' faces. At this point, they can't even drink anymore. Now, they are just dumping water on themselves as their mouths overflow with water. I just kept thinking, "Now they gone throw up all their food they just ate too if this keeps up." Man, that shit was funny, but it wasn't funny to them, I bet. I hope they learned their lesson.

We were issued more ammunition today for our rifles. If I failed to mention, these were not live rounds. They were blanks. I guess the point was for the muscle memory we would need to effectively operate our weapons. No way they give thousands of newly arrived civilians turned soldiers; hundreds of rounds of live ammunition to shoot each other in the ass with. Even still, now I want an assault rifle of my own. I definitely have this on my things to get when I get out of the military list. Well, lights out for now. Let's see what tomorrow brings.

CHAPTER 13

HOW TO BE A SOLDIER 101

1 2/1/09

Today is the first day of December. We officially have 16 days left until we get to go home for Christmas break or winter holidays (a more politically correct term for those sensitive ones), and I, along with the rest of the platoon, can't wait. We woke up to no power surprisingly this morning, so unfortunately, we had to get dressed in the dark, which sucked. On top of that, breakfast fucking sucked too. I hate when a muthafucker fucks up breakfast. It's the most important meal of the day. I wanted to kick the cooks' asses this morning. Served us runny ass "feggs" (fake eggs, you know, the powdered instant shit) and some watery ass meal of oats (doesn't even deserve to be called oatmeal).

We spent the first half of today getting travel arrangements prepared for leave. The travel process itself was simple, what drew it out was a thousand soldiers had to go through it. That's what draws everything out. That's why the army or the military, in general, has a hurry up and wait policy. The quicker you can get in the line for any and everything, the smoother it will go. With so many people doing the same thing and getting processed for the same thing at the same time, honestly, I can't see a better way of doing things because there is no big computer room for everyone to just hop online to do stuff. Uncle Sam is stuck in his ways in this aspect of processing information.

Getting everyone prepared for leave was taking longer than expected, so for lunch, we had some bootleg "Lunch-a-bles" and some cold ass Chef Boyardee. We didn't get to make it to the d-fac (short for dining facility / cafeteria). When you are in basic training, psychologically, you have to cherish the small things and look forward to small victories or pleasures throughout the day. Going to the chow hall was one of my pleasures of the day, as it was for most of us. To have this pleasure taken away was slightly irritating, but realistically, there was nothing I could do about it.

Funny story: I actually got smoked today, and I'll admit it was my fault. I fell asleep. I did, I fell asleep, and I didn't even know it. I was fucking tired, man. The day started early, and I was also done early, so I was in the wait part of the hurry up and wait motto, and it just took over me. All I remember is looking at all the other people falling asleep and getting smoked and laughing, waiting to see who else was going get caught slipping and sleeping (little did I know, we would all get smoked, but I'll get to that later), and then here I am getting a tap on the shoulder. I'm like, "What the fuck?" When did I fall asleep? "You know the drill, on ya feet," Drill Sergeant yelled. I started to speak and was abruptly interrupted with, "Tucker, I watched you for a solid 6 minutes and 13 fucking secs fucking dreaming and nodding. Don't say a word, just drop!" I'm thinking the entire time as I'm doing push-ups, "How the fuck does she see me?" I had a good spot in the corner on the low, very inconspicuous, or so I thought. She didn't drag me, though. She just made me do a few more drills that made me get up. It was mostly to wake me up.

So, we get back to the barracks around 16:00 (4:00 p.m.), and one of the drill sergeants is like, "You guys suck," blah, blah, blah. He had a few privates help pass out new training equipment to replace what was turned in a few days ago from the road march as he continued to tell us how much we sucked. Then he says, "You got 10 minutes to take your shit to the bays and get your ass back down here to the drill pad." When we returned to the pad, another instructor started chewing us out. Telling us how all the other instructors don't have anything good to say about us and going on and on. During his ranting, while we are formed up, he is giving us marching commands. We start marching to this place called "the beach." The beach is as big as a sand pit, similar to the size of a football field. As we approached the "beach," we all started to look at each other. I knew what time it was. Anytime you go to the beach, you are getting what I call "tanned," meaning smoked out. Some people started whispering, and some of the females got nervous and started crying. The crying irritated the males, which caused us to fuss and argue, which then irritated the drill instructors and amplified the whole ordeal.

As everyone else continued to bicker and gripe about the situation, I just mentally prepared for the session as much as I could. You never know how long a smoke session will be, but if you going to the beach, it's not going to be quick and it's not going to be easy. I told myself, "Fuck it, hell, I need the workout. Shit, let's get it then". I knew coming into this I was going to change my entire mental state. I didn't want to go back home the same person I was. Mentally, I had it made up in my mind I was going to be a beast! Period! I wasn't backing down from that. I need to be the best me I can be, so I am all into any physical discipline they want to hand out. On top of that, we were starting to come together as a unit, but it wasn't happening fast enough.

Just as soon as we got to the beach, we dropped and started flutter kicks. All the drill sergeants were there, some contributing to the session and some just spectators. I swear I even saw drill sergeants out there that weren't even a part of my platoon. We got worked pretty well, I will admit. For what seemed to be about an hour, we went from flutter kicking to running in place to push-ups, back to flutter kicks. Of course, the sand makes it tougher, not to mention it gets in everything. The more the females tried to avoid getting dirty, the more exercises we did on the ground, head in the sand. Once we got done in the sand, we went running. I looked at it as intense training, not punishment. In the military, we say sweat is weakness leaving the body. The way we were sweating, we all were going to be rock solid by the end of this. Shit, I enjoyed it mentally once I was able to tune out the drill sergeant's nonsense. I would ignore all the yelling to listen for the next command. We had people try to quit and get jacked up. This one guy tried to run away. You should have seen him putting on juke moves and trying to hurdle trash cans. My thing was, where the hell is he going to run to? We were in South Carolina, and I do believe he was from the mid-west. Even the females got jacked up by other female drill sergeants. Anyone could get it. I'm thinking to myself like what did you expect when you volunteered to join the armed forces?

As I was looking at people getting drug back to the beach from trying to leave and people getting close lined or tacked trying to run away, my boy Covington (big ass ex NC State football player) started to talk. I guess he thought he was going to rally the troops or something. Covington yells out, "They can't smoke us forever, y'all!" As soon as he said that, I knew he had dug a deep grave. As he was about to continue his rally, of course, I heard a drill scream, "Hey, shut the fuck up, and I do mean all the way the fuck up. You don't know shit." Even though Covington was right, there is some stuff you just don't make a public service announcement about. So now we are in a pissing contest with the drill sergeants that, of course, we as the soldiers are going to lose. The instructors made it a point to show us they were boss in all aspects of life for the duration of basic training.

On a psychological level, I'm over the yelling and screaming and vocal intimidation methods being used. I can see right pass that bullshit. I understand why they do it, and I don't blame them. On some level, I may even agree with it being necessary. Some of these kids need discipline, structure, and guidance. Some of them have no one else to look up to or turn to for the structure. They will learn. I just hope it's soon. Until then, I'll have to go through the growing pains with them and hope I can set a positive example.

After the smoke session, it was dinner time. Everyone was starving, as you can imagine, from getting the shit drug out of us at the beach. I can tell I'm getting this 4-minute drill down pat. When we first started and only got 4 minutes to eat, I thought I wasn't going to make it. I thought there was no way in hell anyone could eat a meal in only 4 minutes. Now, I'm able to comfortably, and I pigged out (chicken, mashed potatoes, pasta salad, potato salad, peas, and apple juice). The trick is (now listen up): you must start with the foods easiest to eat, soft foods, and things easy to chew only a few times and swallow. I didn't eat chicken at first because it takes too long to chew and won't leave time for the rest of the food. If you start with the soft foods first, at least if you do run out of time it will be towards the end of the meal and not the beginning. Even eating dinner is a game and mental. I'm learning you must always stay sharp. Every move must be strategic. Even if they would have only given us 2 minutes to eat today, I wouldn't have cared.

Each day I remember why I am here, to help keep me focused on my goals. February 19th is graduation, and I leave for A.I.T. on February 20th. All I have to do is just hang in there until then. Ok, well I must get some rest. Tonight, I have what's called CQ duty. CQ duty is during guard duty hours, but instead of guarding the barracks, you are a drill sergeant assistant for the night duty sergeants on shift. This should be interesting.

12/2/09

Today was a wonderful day! Although nothing spectacular happened, nothing phased me either. We were allowed to sleep an extra 45 minutes today due to PT being canceled. In basic training, an extra 45 minutes of sleep feels like an extra 2 hours. I didn't know what to do with myself. I had a great breakfast (grits, eggs, pancakes, and mixed fruit), and I got to eat it all. You must understand, that whenever you get to eat your entire meal in basic training, that's a victory. Basic training Is not designed to be comfortable, it's the opposite. We are learning how to function effectively in uncomfortable situations (war, everything is all about training to go to war). The sooner people understand that, I think, the better they will be and easier it will be to adjust and adapt (message!).

Ok, so remember when I told you about the haircuts in reception phase when we first arrived? Well, here come the real army cuts.

The skinny, skinny, buzz, buzz. The low-low. The almost bald but I can feel little prickles when I rub my head cuts. So, we all march to the barber shop as a platoon. If you know anything about the barber shop, typically it's not a quick process. And with a platoon full of soldiers to cut, I'm thinking," It's hundreds of people in line. This shit gone take a week to finish." There were about 7 or 8 barbers and from what I could tell they were making bank. From what I gathered in the little shopping center area we were in, there was the post exchange (on post army store like a Wal-Mart) l, the barber shop, and one other store on the other end I couldn't tell what it was. Now let me make this clear: everyone thinks everything is free in the army, absolutely not. All the uniforms come out of your pay, the haircuts that you don't even request come out of your pay, and then you must buy toiletries as well as undergarments. You can't leave, so you have no option but to purchase everything on base.

They charge 2 dollars for the haircuts, which you think is nothing. And how do the barbers live on that? It's because of the mean green oiled machine. This barber shop was designed to have you in and out. Only one style gets cut, and the clippers all have suction hoses (like the vacuum at the car wash). Just low and tight, that's all you get. $2 for a 60-second haircut, that's how long the haircut takes. So, I got to thinking, that's $120 per hour these barbers are making. What other barbers you know make $120 an hour in an average small shop? They don't even have to sweep; they have a suction tank for that too. Everything is always thought through when it comes to Uncle Sam, all possible scenarios.

Of course, by the time we were done with haircuts, it was lunch time. It was a rainy day on and off, but despite the weather, we still had to march everywhere. Drenched in the rain, we still sounded off to the cadences as we marched toward the DFAC.

Drill Sergeant: "Here we go again!"

Soldiers: "Here we go again!"

Drill Sergeant: "Same old shit again!"

Soldiers: "Same old shit again!"

Drill Sergeant: "Marching down the avenue!"

Soldiers: "Marching down the avenue!"

Drill Sergeant: "9 more weeks we're through!"

Soldiers: "9 more weeks we're through!"

It was most exhilarating, I must say. Now, there were still some people bitching and moaning about getting wet. I found the positives in the situation. Yeah, it was wet, but at least it wasn't too cold, so I'll take that (small victories).

There was one cool thing that happened today: we learned how to break down our assault rifles. It's about ten pieces in total, from what I can tell. I don't have it down pat yet, but I'll get it. We worked on assembling and disassembling rifles for hours, up until dinner chow. It kind of reminded me of the scene from "Forrest Gump," when Tom Hanks was assembling his rifle only, I felt more like "Bubba." By now, it was pouring rain outside. You would think we were allowed to wear some type of wet weather gear for the elements, but no, the instructors want to fuck with us more, so we march to chow soaked. I just kept thinking, "It's a game, Tuck, just play the game."

Little did I know, everyone in formation wasn't uniformed, meaning, some people forgot their eye protection while others had their protective glasses on. So, since we all were not alike, you got it, we got smoked! At this point in the game, it's irritating me. Fuck man, we do this every day, we know exactly what to wear every day, every formation, every training exercise. I'm starting to think I'm surrounded by a bunch of morons. Overall, the day was still a good day. I think I'm at the point of starting to enjoy basic training versus just dealing with it.

CHAPTER 14

THERE'S NO I IN TEAM

1 2/3/09

Today was fun as hell. We woke up, went to breakfast, where of course, I enjoyed my ever so delicious pancakes. After breakfast, we all pumped up. Today was obstacle course day. It was somewhat physical, but it was more of a mental course centered around problem solving, critical thinking, and team communication. This course was designed to build faith and trust in each other, and it worked. I actually liked my team members. We didn't argue, not one time, and everyone worked together smoothly. The course lasted most of the day. We ate lunch there and continued the skill building up until about 16:00.

I got my official military identification card today and it's the worst. I look like a freaking ninja turtle. On a brighter note, apparently, word around the barracks is we only have one more week in red phase and then we move on to white phase. Allegedly, there isn't as much yelling in white phase. We shall see, I don't care either way. I'm used to it now and everyone else should be too. I try not to think about the next phase until we get there. Hell, we aren't done with this phase yet, so I say let's just focus on one day at a time.

Funny story: We were moving through the dinner chow line and the lines were long, they twisted and turned in different ways to condense space and move mass amounts of soldiers along efficiently. Usually, there are pivot points on the floor that indicate the direction to turn. One girl made the wrong pivot and a drill instructor noticed. She looked around for a moment to see if anyone saw her. As soon as she took her sigh of relief, boom, he was in her face. I don't even know how he got over there so fast. He chewed her out for a moment, and she did a good job taking it too. Then he said it, "back of the line." You would have thought he told her someone she loved died. She cried so hard. Falling all out on the floor and rolling around. All I could think of was how disgusting that floor was. I just saw some kid spit right around the area she was rolling around in. After a few moments, two other drill instructors came over and picked her up and carried her to the back of the line.

As the days go by, I start to miss home more and more. I feel like I'm missing out on things going on with everyone, but I know I'm not. It's strange how you miss the very place you couldn't wait to get away from. The very place you think is holding you back from whatever dreams you may have.

12/4/09

Well, today was, eh, I don't know how to explain it, mundane, I guess. Not good, but not bad. Not fun, but not hell either. The best part of the day, and the most tiring, was the PT test. I was pumped up for the test because I wanted to see where I was compared to where Uncle Sam wanted me to be. The test consists of 3 sections: 2 minutes of continuous push-ups, 2 minutes of continuous sit-ups, and a 2-mile run finale. I did okay in my class. I did about 56 push-ups, 36 sit-ups, and I ran my 2-mile in 17:26. Of course, the better you do, the higher your score. Everyone is rated based on age and number of push-ups and sit-ups, nothing else. Height nor weight mattered. For the soldiers who were not close to meeting the numbers and times needed, they had additional workouts to help them get to where they needed to be.

For my age bracket, I have to be able to do 47 push-ups, 42 sit-ups, and I must run the 2-mile in under 16:50. To pass the PT test to graduate basic training, you must pass with a 50 core or higher, once you get to A.I.T (Advanced Individual Training), you have to pass with a 60 score. If you can hit the A.I.t numbers coming out of basic training, you will be good to go once you hit your next station.

We started learning land navigation and map reading today. That shit ain't as easy as I thought it was going to be, especially when it comes to identifying plateaus, ridges, and depression, things of that nature. I was amazed at the precision of these maps (I don't know why; they should be accurate; otherwise, they are useless). I think the learning would be more effective if it was in a real setting so you can actually see what a ridge looks like, see what a depression really looks like, and understand what a valley is. We did the book work first and then the application part second. By the time we got to the application part, a lot of people had forgotten what they were looking for.

I'm anxious to get to tomorrow. Tomorrow will be our first recorded "field" day. Field trainings are like extreme camping trips from what I'm hearing. We will train and eat all our meals there. I think it's only one night, but either way, I'm still excited. I'm a city kid, so I have never really been camping before. I assume we are doing this because of the land navigation session we are in. I think it's still going to be fun either way. Any moment I get a chance to relax or chill out, I think about home a lot. Just wondering what's going on back in the "world." Wondering how everyone is doing or what they are up to. I can't believe how ready I am to go home for the holidays. I haven't felt like this since my freshman year in college.

Just thinking about everyone back home is enough to keep me motivated. I didn't want to let my female family and friends down, and I definitely didn't want to get clowned by my home-boys. I heard that Fort Jackson was easy. "Relaxin' Jackson," that's what they call it. I can't tell. I've never "relaxed." I've gotten some shut eye, I've gotten to sit down for a moment, but I've never got that amount of time to relax. Hell, that sounds pretty good. Ok, it is time to hit the hay. I need the rest, plus I have no idea how long the march will be.

12/5/09

A lot is going on in my head today. You know how Jay-Z said, "It was all good just a week ago." Well, it was all good just a few hours ago. We woke up this morning and were supposed to go camping, but the trip got cut short (I'll explain later). We packed all our shit, which ended up being around 70 plus pounds worth of gear, and set out on our 2-mile march. 2 miles doesn't sound too bad, and it wouldn't typically be. The only difference is, we had to carry 70 plus pounds of stuff with us. We set out on the march at 05:30 sharp. I mean, as soon as it struck 05:30, we stepped off. We get to the camp site, and it's still dark as hell outside. We scoured the area to find a good place to set up camp and were instructed to erect our tents. The tents were one-man tents that we were issued during the reception phase, and I absolutely love it! It's designed perfectly to preserve heat and regulate the temperature inside the tent to be comfortable for one. "Definitely keeping this when I get out," was the first thing I thought after completing my setup.

My battle buddy and I helped set each other's tent up, then we went to get breakfast. I thought we were just going to grab a few MREs which would've sucked, but undenounced to me, we were actually having a hot breakfast. I was mad originally this morning because I thought we were going to the chow hall this morning (you know how I am about my flap jacks). Lo and behold, to my surprise, we had grits, eggs, and what do you know, freakin' pancakes (hot damn)! After breakfast, we split up by platoons and spent the day going through different tactical stations. The first station was focused on hand signals during road marches and different march formations. We learned how to signal to form wedge formations, staggered columns, and straight-line formations. We also went through scenarios when you would expect to use each formation. Station two was badass. This station was focused on enemy fire and how to react. We learned how to properly drop and return fire and how to move in alpha and bravo teams. This is the J.I. Joe shit I was waiting for. Learning these maneuvers made a bunch of us feel a little more comfortable about being equipped and ready for combat situations. From return fire, we went to learning how to spot cover under fire and moving in what's called a "bounding" technique to the nearest cover. This stage was where I could tell the physical training was going to come in handy because it was a lot of crawling and dragging and sprinting. Last was road stops and checks. We learned how to search vehicles, what to look for, how to spot signs or suspicions of travelers involved in terrorist activities, and a few more things. I had a ball!

After lunch was the bummer. We were informed we would have to leave early due to a forecast of snow headed our way. So, instead of more training, we spent the rest of the afternoon packing up our shit. I'm thinking, "Here, in the Carolinas, no way." I knew it wasn't going to snow, but I was glad we returned for two reasons. Reason one: I forgot some things I was supposed to bring. These were important items because they were warm weather sleep gear I knew I'd need for the night. Reason two: I didn't want to eat another MRE for dinner. We arrived back to our part of the base just in time to catch the last wave of dinner chow.

Here's where the downward spiral thing starts. We get back to the surprise of mail! I was excited because I thought I would definitely be getting a letter today. I wrote everybody so I just knew I'd have at least one letter. I waited and the drill sergeant called every name but mine. He was calling people I never even heard of or knew were in our platoon but didn't call mine. Muthafucka! I was a little down for a minute, I'll admit that. So at that point, I was like, "I ain't writing no more letter til' I get some replies." This is the part where basic training feels like jail. In basic training, mail is sacred. Everyone looks forward to receiving mail because mail is the only connection you have to the outside world. When I don't get mail, I feel as if I'm being robbed of that connection. But, enough wallowing, chin up on to the next day.

12/6/09

I think we as a platoon, had another breakthrough today. Today may be the first day we resembled soldiers. We all made it to formation on time, uniformed, and ready to sound off at a moment's notice. There was word going around that the drill sergeants were thinking of keeping us in red phase for another week. That's embarrassing; no platoon wants to be held back in any phase. You always want to progress. Would you want to be held back a grade in school? No way we could let that happen. We all got together this afternoon and had a heart to heart with each other to figure out how we all can come together and get through this training. There are so many immature people in my platoon. Then again, there are a lot of kids in basic training in general. There are so many different attitudes, no one wants to listen to anyone else talk, and everyone wants to be the boss.

With the bays not being co-ed, of course, we, the guys, decided to meet with the girls because enough was enough. Everyone has their own personal reasons why the Army was the best decision for them at this time in their life. With that being said, we all need to do what we have to do so that we can do what we want to do. I just hope that sometime tonight, while everyone is sleeping, a light bulb goes off in everyone's head, and tomorrow we have our shit together.

Anyway, today was pretty chill because it's Sunday. Sunday usually is cleaning day, outside and inside the bays. I wanted to go to church but that extra hour and a half of sleeping is almost impossible to pass up. Sunday cleaning is all about getting ready for Mondays. Mondays are the worst by far. 05:00 is here before you know it and everything is "Go, Go, Go, Move, Move, Move!" Mondays will always challenge your mental toughness. The good thing is this is our last full week before we leave for the holidays. Word is we are going to the gas chamber this week at some point. Not too sure how I feel about this gas chamber. They may be taking this training a bit too far now.

I was able to get a lot done today. Hopefully, I can go right to bed when lights out come. I must admit, there is more I can do to be a better soldier and I'm getting there. I know it won't come overnight, but it will never come if I don't apply myself. I had a few bunkmates help me with rifle breakdown and cleaning. I got most of it except one part in the upper receiver that I got stuck with regarding the firing pin. Sorry for being a bit incohesive with the writing, my brain is all over the place. Hopefully, I'll get mail soon. Hell, I'd love to hear from anyone at this point.

12/7/09

Today was cool. I think it's safe to say we are starting to come together. It's probably because these muthafuckas are starting to realize they don't want to be stuck in red phase of all of basic training. We did more land navigation classes, and tomorrow we will go back to the field for more knowledge application. From my understanding, the points that we plotted today are the points we will have to find tomorrow. Word is, the drill sergeants will drive us out to the middle of nowhere, and we will have to use the coordinates to find our way back. I hope my teammates have been paying attention in class because I have no idea if the instructors are coming to pick us up. In the briefing, they said we were to report to a certain sergeant when we arrived back. I'm excited; I feel pretty good about my navigational skills so far.

I got my first letter today! Surprisingly, it wasn't from anyone I wrote to, it was from my boy Herb! Herb got my address from my boy DJ, whom I did write. It's crazy because even though I didn't hear from whom I wanted, I heard from exactly who I needed to hear from. Herb was a soldier, so he knew what I was going through and was going to go through. I appreciated that. To be honest, that letter was all I needed, and I didn't even know it.

12/8/09

Today was a very trying day! I think I hate being in the first platoon! Just when I think things are good or starting to be good, or I have high hopes, these fuckers do something stupid to make me regret it all. There are way too many immature kids that I can't get away from. Sometimes I just want to choke the shit out of them. And it's the little 18,19,20-year-old punks. This one kid (I won't call his name), just for the life of him, could not stop talking in formation. Rule number one: NO TALKING IN FORMATION! I mean, how fucking hard is that concept to shut what is known as the FUCK up. Then there's this other freaking idiot (I won't mention his name even though I should so his mom can know how much of a failure she was) who keeps making these damn tweedy bird noises or some shit. That shit is annoying as fuck. I know they get mad and turn all red when I tell them, "Yo, shut the fuck up!" Fuck it, I know none of them bitches can whoop my ass anyway, so on some level, I don't care. Then there's this dumb ass, country ass back creek dude (whom I won't name). I mean like Rocky 2 can't read the teleprompter dumb. Keeps talking and making jokes in formation. Won't shut the fuck up! These are the assholes that get us "smoked" all the time.

Take earlier today for instance, Dumb ass wants to be Mr. funny man and knock another soldier's weapon on the ground, so they would have to do push-ups (rule number one when handling your weapon, DON'T DROP IT!). Instead of just him having to do push-ups, we all had to drop. Now everyone is getting smoked on some "fuck boy" shit. I swear I wanted to smack the shit out of this guy. The sad part about it all is all the instructors have said over and over again to stop with the stupid shit, and here we are with idiots still doing the dumb shit. This is why we will never get out of red phase. Not the way we are going. I really want to look into getting switched to another platoon. I don't even know if there is such a thing, and I damn sure ain't starting this shit over. The only thing the entire company is full of fuck ups.

So, tomorrow is the big gas chamber day. I'm excited about it, but then again, I don't know. We tried on our gas mask today and I don't feel as if mine fit properly. They are talking about I may have to share one. Eww, that's fucking gross, take a mask from someone that's been breathing and slobbering all in it from gas, no way. Oh, you're going to love this, another funny story today. So, we went to morning formation. After formation, we come back to the bay to find the entire bay trashed! I mean, vandalized! Bunks overturned, lockers turned over and trashed, washing powder dumped all over people's clothes and linen. Some of the drill instructors even sprayed shaving cream all over the bay floors, spelling out, "clean up all this shit." We all were looking around like, "What the fuck?" Luckily, all my shit was good. Now instead of 2 people on fire guard, they made four people do fire guard, so you know what that means: less shifts to rotate so now that's less sleep for everyone. With four people on each hour, now we all have guard duty every night, depending on where you are in the rotation. Some nights, you may have it twice. On that note, let me get some shut eye. My shift starts at midnight.

CHAPTER 15

I, I, I, I'M STAYIN' ALIVE

1 2/9/09

Wow! All I can say is today was crazy! Today was a day I most certainly will never forget. The gas chamber. Oh lord, the gas chamber is a muthafucka boy, I swear! It really is indescribable to put the feeling into words, but I'll try my best. Before I get to the chamber, let's start with wake up. When we woke up, we immediately got dressed and went to formation. But instead of heading to breakfast, we marched set out on a road march to the gas chamber. Once we got there, we ate breakfast (which was really lunch food. Freakin' MREs). Everyone was ordered to eat something to ensure each soldier had food on their stomach. One drill sergeant told us it was to make sure when we vomited, we weren't dry heaving and something actually was coming out. Once we all got an MRE, we were instructed to grab a patch of grass (have a seat) and listen to a safety briefing regarding the chamber and what to expect.

The instructors started out by letting us know up front, this was probably going to be the most uncomfortable day we were going to have in basic training. Immediately, everyone's face went to "Oh shit." They explained the type of gas we were going to be inhaling as well as the effects they would have on us and for how long. Some of the effects described were tingling sensations, slight/mild cases of coughing, slight irritation of the eyes, and some may experience a runny nose. The purpose in the gas chamber is to get you to trust in your equipment and what it is designed to do. It's designed to keep you focused and calm in small scaled chemical warfare scenarios and it is to get you adjusted to functioning and operating under the most undesirable and unfavorable conditions.

Once the instructors were done with their briefing, we were instructed to get our masks out and hold them up above our heads. The army does everything in an elementary style so there are no confusions and to make sure everyone was prepared for the training. Once a drill instructor cleared each soldier and made sure everyone had a mask, we were all instructed to put our masks on and make sure our filters worked. I was nervous. I can't believe the time was here. I mean, dang, I was ready, but fuck that was mostly talk. Everyone is ready until it's time to get to it. The instructor asked for the first 15 volunteers. The way it works is, if no one volunteers, then you get volun-told. Fuck it, man, may as well go on and get it over with. Fuck it. "I'll go, drill sergeant," I screamed out. I'd rather be first than last. "Tucker, my mutherfucker, way to take the lead soldier," one of my platoon sergeants said before patting me on the back. Plus, I figured everyone else would be so nervous and paying attention to not trying to go. They wouldn't be paying attention to us when we came out, and that would allow me the time to watch everyone else as they came out. Not only that, but I figured by the time others come out, I'll be over whatever effects we would have.

We lined up and all moved hesitantly toward the gas house. As we approached, you could smell the gas lingering from probably about 50 to 60 yards away. The crazy thing about that was, we were the first group of the morning so whatever smell we were smelling, came from the previous day. The gas house, or gas chamber, is a big log cabin-style house that I believe had 3 or 4 rooms in it from what I could see. As we got to the door, the instructor told us to file in from the right, stop at arm's length away from the person in front of us, and face to the center of the room. There was this slight peppery stench in the air, but I just figured it was engraved in the walls from all of the exercises ran there through all the different platoons that get cycled through. What I didn't realize until we were all inside was that some of us went to the room to the right, and some of us went to the room to the left. The third room was the instructor's room. It kind of reminded me of like an interrogation room with the two-way mirror and all, except that we could see the instructors standing behind the glass watching us. The final room was the gas room where they administered the gas and ran the simulators.

"Ok, listen up everyone," yelled the instructor. "Everyone place your mask over your heads and make sure they are firmly secured to your faces." Once we all did that, we were instructed to give a high thumbs up with our right hand. "Once the gas flows in, do not, and I repeat, do not freak out." Of course, that's a disclaimer that someone is going to freak out. "Once the room is full and visibility is close to zero, you will be instructed to remove your breathing equipment. If you do not remove your breathing equipment, we will remove it for you." Shit got real and really quick. "Once your mask is removed, you will be asked a series of questions by your drill sergeants you must answer. Once you finish answering all of your drill instructors' questions, you will collectively recite the soldier's creed. Is that understood?" "Hoah!" we all sounded off. "On my countdown, the gas will be released, and you are not to leave prior to being released. If you try to run out, you will regret it. The only way out, is to push forward. Ready in 5,4,3,2.." Then out of nowhere, BOOM!

Oh shit! Out of nowhere, this blast shook my soul like a big ass bass speaker box. It rattled a few of us and then, before you knew it, smoke was everywhere. I heard the canisters being released, but after a minute or so, it got so smokey. I seriously could only make out shapes. After another 30 seconds or so, nothing, pure white. Like you are smack in the middle of a cloud, and you are a big ass toxic smoke cloud. I literally could not see my hand in front of my face. But I heard the loudspeaker. "Soldiers, you are to remove your mask. As you remove your mask, you are to keep your eyes open and breathe normally." I couldn't even get my mask up past my mouth before I started coughing up my lungs. "Tucker, I need you to tell me what unit you're in, the name of all three of your drill instructors, and the city and state you are from, go." I'm thinking to myself as I'm regurgitating the information requested and gasping for air at the same time, "Where the fuck is this muthafucker and how the fuck can he see me?" By this time, my eyes were burning furiously like someone was pouring flaming hot sauce in my eyes, nose was running like a water faucet. It was horrible. Definitely unbearable. All I could think was can we please hurry up and get out of here. It felt like time was standing still. Then it happened.

We were probably about two or three people down the line reciting all the information when it happened. The sergeant said, "Whatever you do, don't freak out, and don't run." "Oh sergeant, oh lord sergeant, help me," I hear dumb ass screaming to the left of me. "Take it easy soldier, relax," drill sergeant stated. (Gasp for air) "I can't breathe, oh drill sergeant, I can't breathe, I gotta go, aw no, I gotta go," dumb ass starts screaming. "You can't breathe because you're trying to hold your breath private. Now relax and follow the fucking direction soldier, and snap out of it. You are fucking embarrassing yourself!" drill sergeant screamed. By this point, everyone else had moved on to reciting the "Soldiers Creed," but we had all stopped to watch the spectacle dumbass was putting on. Even the other instructors stopped to watch. "No, no, no, I gotta go, I gotta go," screams dumbass. "We got a runner," yelled one of the instructors. Out of nowhere comes this clothesline from another drill sergeant who was close by. Next thing you know, dumbass was balled up quick. We all were marched out of the gas chamber, instructed to breathe and flap our arms as we were leaving. Meanwhile, dumbass was being carried out hogtie style for trying to run. Fucking idiot, I told that mutherfucka to keep cool, everyone did, and now look at him. He's never going to live this down once we get back to the bays.

As we all filed out of the gas house, coughing, crying, and gaging some vomiting, all I could think was, "I'm glad I got that over. I'm never doing that shit again, and let me hurry up and get right so I can laugh at everyone else coming out that's about to go through it." All in all, the chamber session was about 10 to

15 minutes for each group, but it took all day to recover. The immediate burn and irritation lasted for about 15 minutes after release from the chamber, but some of the effects lasted the remainder of the day. One of the drill instructors told me that they taped the gas house session. I'm definitely going to have to buy a copy of this tape because that shit was funny in hindsight. Well, shit, that was enough for today. I don't think I can even take it anymore. I know dumbass can't take no more. I bet that'll teach him to shut the fuck up.

12/10/09

Let me just say, that today was a very trying day. Drill sergeants were really getting on my nerves. Once again, nobody in the platoon listens, and I just think that everybody is tired of everyone else. Drill sergeants are tired of us "privates," and we are definitely tired of them. Mentally, it's a lose-lose situation for us as trainees. We had the worst instructors on duty today. I hate those cocksuckers. All they do is down-talk us, like we are shit, like we disgust them; not in a drill sergeant "I'm just yelling and screaming" kind of way, but more so in a personal way. I don't know why I feel like this because they don't really know each of us on a personal level like that yet. But nevertheless, I do have those feelings. I can see it in their eyes. Every chance they get, something negative comes out of their mouths. There is never anything remotely close to positivity.

Then, the little fat one says something to the effect of, "You don't deserve to have that American flag patch on your sleeve," and "We should be ashamed because people died for us to wear that patch. I'm thinking, "Fuck you, dude!" Just like they placed themselves in harm's way, we signed up to do the same damn thing. He pissed me off with that shit. I feel he should've at least respected the fact that we volunteered for this. A lot of those other soldiers he was referencing were drafted. I will admit he did have some validity within some of the points he was trying to make. That still doesn't change the fact that they talk to us like shit. It's demoralizing. Listen, I understand there are a lot of kids here, but I'm a man, and I'm a man before I'm a soldier. So now, my mentality is," I don't have shit to say to those cocksucker muththafuckas."

On top of the drill sergeants, don't forget, we have people who just refuse or find it impossible to shut up in formation or in class. Some were not listening or paying attention. This one little shitbag had the nerve to fire a fucking round off (blank ammunition, but in basic training, that's considered live) in the barracks. I guess he thought he would get away with it because no one was around. This situation really made the drill sergeants mad, so of course, they smoked the hell out of us. We got smoked until someone confessed, and that took hours. I mean, not a damn thing went right today, not one. Now I'm thinking I'll be glad when basic training is over.

Let's make this clear. In no way at this point have I felt like maybe I made the wrong decision. I'm just ready to be done with basic training. The frustration level is at a high right now with my platoon, and we have had a few soldiers think about going AWOL (absent without leave). That's the worst thing they could do. Not only will they not get released from their contract (in most cases), but they will get recycled through basic training, meaning they will have to start from day one again (after doing this shit, that's definitely not an option most of us would consider), they also will get an article-15 discipline statement added to their permanent file. Let me break this part down for you in short terms and civilian terms. Getting an article-15 charge in the military is like getting a charge in the real world. The more serious offenses will require a court martial, and you will go to military jail, and some will require extra duty (like community service), not to mention you will lose any little bit of rank you may have or will get in the near future.

The mental exhaustion is just as intense as the physical training. Every bit as intense. Everything about you is in the transformation stage. Mind and body. Until this clicks in everyone, and all of us understand to embrace the change to be a better person, it's going to stay exhausting. Hopefully, tomorrow will be a better day. For now, I'm just glad this day is a done deal.

12/11/09

Today, nothing special happened. Nothing bad happened either, so with that being said, then it was a good day. I guess everyone is mentally drained from yesterday. Drill instructors, and soldiers, we all have had enough of the emotional rollercoaster, so I think today was about hitting the reset button. We are all antsy about going home in a few days. Like a school kid counting down until the last day before summer break. I finally got a letter from my sister today. I would normally be excited about mail, but today I ran on empty when it came to the emotion tank. That's all for now, maybe tomorrow will be adventurous. We shall see.

12/12/09

Today was a good day. It was cold as hell (for the Carolinas), like 32 degrees. Guess how we started the day? Running. Yup, cold as hell, and we start by breaking a sweat. We split up into our groups (A, B, and C groups based on physical ability), did our warm up exercises, then proceeded to run a mile. After physical training, we had review sessions for the Basic Combat Training Life Skills test. The test is on Monday, and if you don't pass, you risk the chance of getting recycled through basic training. We used test dummies for our demonstrations of life saving techniques. The techniques included making and applying tourniquets, being able to acknowledge signs and symptoms of shock, treating gunshot wounds, and more. My favorite part was the scenario for punctured lung patients.

We learned a lot and reviewed a lot. I think things started to set in for a few of us (I know some things sank in for me today). The reality is, we may need to use these techniques. These are real life scenarios some of us WILL be in. The only difference is there was no blood. We were instructed to scream as if we were really in pain and as if our life depended on it. The screaming created distractions that affected some's thought process (exactly what it was supposed to do). These techniques are for stressful situations. In most of the situations, I wouldn't wish on my worst enemy (even though I don't have known enemies). Most of the scenarios are life saving scenarios, and the soldier needs immediate medical attention to keep them ALIVE until medics get there.

Being that most of us are not going to be medics, and most of the soldiers around us in these situations won't be medics, the solutions aren't ideal as if you were in a hospital, but they work, and working is ALWAYS better than not working. Prime example is, in the event that CPR is needed and chest compressions need to be performed, it's a good chance a rib may break and a lung may puncture. Then you ask yourself, "Am I okay with them having a broken rib or punctured lung, or do I want them to die?" Same question if it was yourself in the scenario. For me, I'm taking the broken rib; at least I'll live.

For some reason, all the drill sergeants were cool today. Not much screaming and yelling, and there was compassion being displayed. This feeling and observation also confirmed that this training was important. I think maybe this is why they laid off of us. I know my instructors were the real deal. I knew they were battle-tested, and maybe some of it was still sensitive for them and brought up memories they didn't want to remember. But they wanted to make sure we remembered this part. Maybe they knew, now wasn't the time for the yelling, and the compassion probably came from past experiences. I mean, not one drill instructor snapped or got irritated. They all took as long as we needed to grasp the concept. Some even told stories of how they messed up and how they weren't perfect when they were in basic training either. I had a drill sergeant I thought didn't even know I existed call me by name and tell me how he saw the growth in me. I was for sure this guy had no idea who I was up until this point. Yet here he is, giving me examples up until now of how I have changed. Even when you think no one is watching, they indeed are watching.

I'm hearing talks about getting ready to move to white phase. The instructors keep hinting at it during training. Man, I hope so. I hear as the phases progress, the drill instructors ease up a bit. But hey, this is basic training, as soon as you think you have something figured out, Bang, they change the game on you. Maybe they won't this time. Maybe this time we earned it. Maybe this time we have shown permanent growth and not just a few good days. We got news that one of the drill instructors was leaving permanently next week. That was some of the best news of the day. When we heard, everyone had a little grin on their face. This drill sergeant was one of, if not the worst one. Yeah, I think we are going to white phase. I think they may be sending him to a new group to give them hell now. Lights out now. Not too bad of a Saturday.

12/13/09

I feel like I was robbed of my Sunday. Fuck! Sundays are the only days we get to sleep in a little bit. Typically, we get to sleep in until about 07:00-07:30. This Sunday, we were woken up at 05:45 on some bullshit, and we had a lot of shit to do. Breakfast was kick-ass, but lunch and dinner were bullshit. We had this safety briefing about what not to do when we go home for leave. Don't drink and drive, don't hit your spouse. Basically, don't show your ass when you go home since you haven't been home in a while.

Just to drive the point home, the military invited a mother to come speak to us about how she lost her eldest son due to a car accident he was behind the wheel of. I'll admit, it was a touching story, and the speaker was a strong lady. She allowed pictures from the crash scene to be shown as a part of her engagement. I can't imagine reliving that over and over with different training classes. Maybe she is used to it by now. I don't know how anyone can get used to that, though.

This week should be fairly easy, I'm assuming. From what I'm hearing, all we are doing is getting haircuts, packing things to take home (mostly civilian things we won't need anymore), and there is this reflection session we are to have with our platoon drill sergeants. I can't wait for the reflection session. We get to talk about likes and dislikes, how we feel we have grown, and more or less, a time to reassure and uplift one another. While I am excited for the pow-wow session, I can't wait to get away from some of these dumbasses for a while. Okay, well, I have a fire guard tonight plus an early start for test day tomorrow. Lights out for me.

12/14/09

Today was really fun. We had combat medical training where we did a wounded soldier rescue mission while under simulated fire. We worked in two-man teams, one in the place of the wounded soldier, the other the rescuer. Once the wounded partner was rescued, aid needed to be administered according to the scenario. I love field exercises; they get us ready for real life scenarios. They also drive home the severity of these situations.

After the field training exercises, we had our combat survival written test. The test went over situations involving collapsed lungs due to punctures, gunshot wounds, broken bones, burns, and medical evacuation procedures (medevac). I've learned so much over the past few days with this training. I feel confident in my team members and my own abilities in the event I needed to help. Tomorrow is the last day of training before we start heading home. We have a PT test tomorrow morning. I can't wait to take mine. I've been training hard (on a personal level) so mentally, I'm ready to blow this thing out of the water. The only thing is, on company PT test day, wake up is at 04:00. I did get a letter today from my homegirl Jennifer. That was unexpected but a pleasant surprise. I still haven't received anything from Shakira or Monica, I don't know, maybe they forgot. I know everyone has their own problems and life to live.

Tomorrow is the first day we get paid. We have been here a month and haven't been paid yet. Not like it really matters, we can't go anywhere to buy anything, and you pay for food and shelter with blood, sweat, and tears. Whoever came up with the idea that the army gives free hots and a cot had no idea what the hell they were talking about. It's all good though, I get to go home with a little bit of money in my pocket. The very first thing I'm going to do is buy myself a good meal and eat as slow as I possibly can, savor the flavor. The one thing we don't have time to do in training is properly dine. As they say in basic training, "Eat now and taste it later."

I told one of my drill sergeants I would continue to work out over the break, and that is exactly what I intend to do. Our lieutenant colonel gave this wack-ass speech about how we must contact our battle buddy every 72 hours to make sure they are not doing any dumb shit to get arrested. I'm like, "Bullshit! Seventy-two hours after I get back, I'm going to be fucked up." Ok, well, lights out. Tomorrow is an early day and a long one.

12/15/09

Just as I thought, today we did much of nothing. Wake up was at 03:30, surprisingly, I wasn't tired. We did our PT test today and at first, I wasn't feeling it. Then I remembered how much I had riding on it and quickly mustered up some energy to carry on with the fitness ceremonies. I was ecstatic to find my run time had improved by over a minute since the last time we did a test about ten days ago. After PT, we formed up for my favorite part of the day: breakfast. Once we broke out of formation, I was the first back in the barracks to shower and change. I hear in white phase, there is more time allotted for sleeping and eating. I can't wait for that.

The rest of the day was spent cleaning equipment and weapons for turn-in, cleaning the bays, and finishing up leave preparations for Thursday. We had another safety briefing, this time it was with the first sergeant. Once again, he drilled it in our heads about sex, drugs, and doing either of them while driving. "Let the other person drive, let them get the DUI," is what we were instructed. Now, it's down to the hurry up and wait time before leave. I'm sure tomorrow will be nothing but waiting for buses to leave. Nothing to write until I return. I'm going to do civilian shit. Who knows when the next time will be that I get to.

CHAPTER 16

I THINK THIS IS WHITE PHASE

1 /03/10

Today was the return to base after the holiday leave. I must say, the leave was much appreciated and much needed. The leave overall was a sign of relief. I was able to do everything I said I wanted to do, plus some. I didn't get to spend as much time with my sisters Joy and Shakira and my niece Janiya. My sisters were upset with me. In the same breath, I can understand how they feel, and it saddens me. Bottom line is there just weren't enough hours in the days to go around and spend time with everyone. Hell, there were some people I didn't get to see at all. As I say all that, it also makes me feel good too. It lets me know that they love me and miss me.

I spent a few days with my sister Lisa, but mostly, I was at my friend Monica's house. I thought by staying there, it would give us a good chance to rebuild our friendship. This year, we kind of fell off (after I got arrested, long story). I really value her as a friend and I want to strengthen our bond. I think my relationship with my sister will get better too. Maybe the distance between us is helping with that. Now that I'm nestled in my bunk after a nice shower, I still don't regret my decision to join the armed forces. I'm ready to give these last six weeks all I have. I need this in a way, like everyone needs their personal calling. It's funny how this training is making me think about life in general. I'm focused on so many tasks at hand. Focused on finishing basic training, focused on my time management, and focused on making a better life for myself.

01/04/10

Today was pretty good, considering it was the first full day back in the swing of things. For some reason, a lot of people weren't feeling it. Some were in low spirits, and I assume it's because they miss civilian life. Going back home and seeing family and friends will do that to you. Remembering what you had and what you left or gave up can make people have second thoughts.

Then again, some were like, "I don't know if this army life is for me." I can understand that as well. Some of this shit you wouldn't know to ask about. Some of this shit you just have to go through to understand. As for me, I have too many things I want to do and accomplish. Plus, you only live once.

It may sound crazy, but even through all the emotions we go through, I think it's all fun. Being outside freezing your ass off, being stressed out at times. Mixing it up with everyone, all of the different obstacles and adventures; to me, that's living life. Being able to embrace the ups and downs, enjoying the ride. That's the fun part, to be able to look back one day and say, "Hey, I did this and I did that, and it was crazy!" Moving on, today we didn't do too much. We were reassigned our rifles and did a lot of rifle cleaning. Tomorrow starts the real fun for the next few weeks. We start weapons training. Gunplay, the gangster's paradise. Learning how to become a professional killer. All day, every day, will be about us becoming one with our killing machines at the range. How sweet is that? I don't look forward to eating all these MREs all day, but hey, I'll take it if it means I get to let off rounds all day. We got the official word from the drill sergeants that we are moving to white phase in the next few days. I don't believe in shit until shit happens, though. So far, so good.

Leaving home was a bittersweet feeling. I saw people I missed and road around my city for a bit, just soaking it in. I missed my friends and loved ones. As I looked at my neighborhood, I also saw knuckleheads, dope dealers, trash on the ground, and cops everywhere. That confirmed for me the reason I left. I didn't want to be the same guy in the same spot, standing still, being broke. Riding on the west side down Remount Rd and West Boulevard, riding down Sugar Creek Rd seeing prostitutes and homeless people convinced me I deserved better. So, better I will get for myself.

01/05/10

Well, today was CRAZY! Let me start by saying, it was cold as hell out this bitch. When I say cold, I mean shivering cold! Can't feel my hands or nose type cold. We were up at 04:30 outside and ready to go. The first thing I thought was, of course, " This is bullshit!" We stood outside in the cold for about two and a half hours just to walk into the CQ office just to sign some initials on a piece of paper to go to the range. What the fuck else is there to sign? I have been here for a while now, we all have. Hell, we joined the Army; that should be all the initialing needed. Once we got all that nonsense out of the way and started the road march to the range, the day was fun as hell.

Firing that M-16 was amazing! I was disappointed a little bit because I didn't successfully group my shots, but I still thought it was awesome. The groups of rounds have to be within a 4 centimeter diameter from 25 yards away. Tomorrow, we are going to a virtual range to shoot. The drill sergeant says this is all we will be doing for the next three weeks is weapons operations. If this is what the rest of basic is going to be like, I think the time is going to fly by. I am a little worried though because you have to successfully group your rounds to graduate from basic training.

Okay, so that was the great part of the day; the not-so-great part was mail call. It's funny because we, as soldiers, look forward to mail. I got a letter from Joy today, but as soon as I opened it up, thinking happy thoughts, I read about how she and Shakira were mad at me. I'm thinking I don't need the extra stress with every-thing we go through here. I was already down because I couldn't spend as much time with them as I would have liked. Now, the letter just rubbed it in more. Just when I thought a relationship had been strengthened with Monica and me, now I feel as if a relationship is dwindling. I feel like I can't win for losing. It's hard having to communicate with people through letters. Response time takes too long, and too much information can be misconstrued trying to make a point. I'm trying not to let home affect me too much so I can continue to do what I need to do. On that note, time for some shut eye, fire guard shift calling me at midnight.

01/06/10

Today was pretty fun, not quite as fun as I expected, but still a fun day. We did go to the electronic range, but it was different than what I was thinking it would be. First off, we only got to take six shots (3 in each clip). The simulator was almost like a futuristic Nintendo Duck Hunt game. Instead of shooting ducks, there were planes. Then there was this analytical breakdown of each shot on the computer. I didn't even know that there was so much to analyze. The system analyzed aim tendencies, trigger squeeze tendencies, shot anticipation, trajectory, you name it. It even analyzed how long you hold the trigger squeeze (aka your follow-through). The experience was fascinating; it just didn't last long. We did more waiting in line and anticipation than we did firing shots.

We got a new drill sergeant today to replace the asshole that left. That means before you know it, graduation will be here. There is not one day we don't think about graduation. I got my first letters today from Dani Cakes (Danielle) and Monica. That made me smile. Even though I knew they were coming, they still made me smile. Okay, moving along. Don't want to get too mushy. Basic training up to this point has been interesting to say the least. I'm trying to paint the picture as clearly as I can, as detailed as I can, but there are still so many feelings and emotions that change at a moment's notice. I'm not sure if it is even possible to remember and convey everything. There are some I'm sure I'm forgetting about.

You would be surprised that with so many people around and so many things going on, just how lonely it can get. I thank God for keeping me strong through it all. There are only a few people in my life that I know understand what I'm going through. Three in particular, my homeboys Kyle, Jason, and Herb (they all served). Another thing that's crazy is, that the people I do this for don't even realize I do it for them or what I go through. I even surprise myself with some of the things I put up with here. My fingers are still numb from being out in the cold for so long. There are still a few things I need to block out of my mental space that are still affecting me. Like that letter Joy sent me the other day. I think all that bullshit affects training. Doesn't really help me thinking about the "real world" and I'm not there. Shakira told me at one point, "It's hard to have female friends because of all of the catfights." Ok, lights out. Need all my energy for tomorrow.

1/07/10

Oh my goodness, today was the shit! In fact, this entire week so far has been fun as hell. We went back to the rifle range for the entire day. The only thing I didn't enjoy was eating those damn MREs for breakfast. Who wants penne pasta for breakfast? Not this guy. I'm from the south. This guy needs grits and eggs. This guy needs biscuits, pancakes, and some kind of meat. The other good news is I passed my shot grouping for the marksman test. I believe I went over this before, but in case you forgot, the grouping session is when we have to place 6 out of 10 shots in a 4 centimeter diameter, which is about the size of a typical hand-held flashlight ring. Like this:

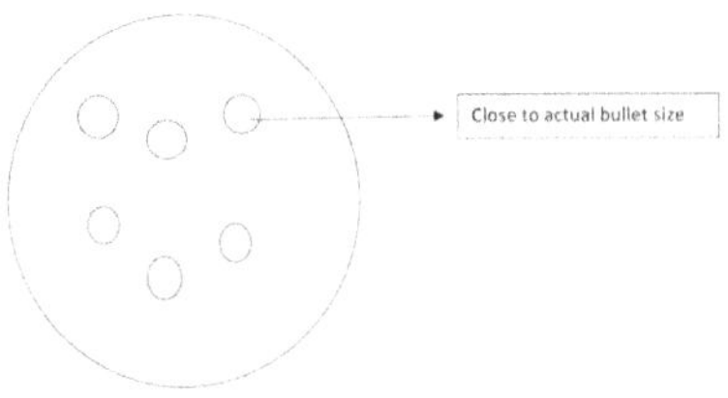

Keep in mind this is from 25 meters away. I must admit, I think that's pretty impressive. I'm going to be surgical with this bitch before it's all said and done. This is what I mean when I say you can't teach this stuff to any and everyone. Some guys from where I'm from are already too hot-tempered, let alone teach them how to properly shoot. Not all that Hollywood stuff. No way! You get the average shooter in the civilian world and put them against the average military shooter, civilians will lose every time. Just the sheer repletion and muscle memory of shooting, all soldiers have. It becomes instinctive. Spending hours and hours at a time at the range with basically an unlimited source of ammunition (literal truckloads), how could you not get good? We have this big road march coming up that I'm excited about. We're headed to a big boy range. Can't wait to see how this range will be set up.

It feels like the past four days have been more like two days. Everything is moving so fast now. I got a few more letters in from Monica and Danielle, but they were old. These letters were received on base after we all had gone home for the holidays. I still read them, knowing the details that would lie within the writing. I just like getting mail. Moving on. I have the early fireguard shift tonight. That means I get a full night's sleep uninterrupted. That's huge!

Okay, here we go. Funny story time. Remember the Latino guy I said I didn't like? Well, he got into a heated argument with one of the drill instructors today while we were at the range. We were up next to shoot after devouring chow and he had to use the latrine (bathroom/porter-potty). He asked the drill sergeant if he could use the bathroom and the drill sergeant said no. Told him he had time during chow and he should've gone during chow before he came back to the live(active fire) side of the range. Well, he didn't like that answer and refused to go back inside the range. Why did he do that? The drill sergeant snapped after that. He got so close to the soldier's face, that I thought they were going to kiss. Yelling and screaming. So my peer goes into defense mode, starts screaming back at the drill sergeant and shit. "I ain't scared of you!" he screams out. Now I'm just looking to see if the drill sergeant gone kick his ass. "Fuck it!" I thought to myself. I didn't like the little boy anyway.

Drill sergeant, of course, smokes the fuck out of the soldier, but the worse part, in my opinion, was the aftermath of that argument. Every time we went to chow the rest of the day, he got sent to the back of the line. Drill sergeant would purposely look for him and walk up to him, stand there for a minute with a blank face, spit his tobacco dip out, and say in a disgusted tone, "Back of the line." We all were hungry, but damn, to be the last one to eat all day has to suck. Other than that, today is over. One more day closer to the end. One day stronger, one day more of experience. I'll let you know how this road march goes tomorrow.

1/08/10

To tell the truth, I'm kind of disappointed. Today was interesting. Not quite what I expected, but still fun, though. We were supposed to do this huge road march that I was super excited about. We did do the road march, but it wasn't long at all. I didn't feel challenged in any way. It was cold all day, and this morning was actually the warmest part of the day, so I felt like it was perfect conditions for the long march.

On a bright note, I discovered that my weapon wasn't zeroed properly, which contributed to some inaccuracies in my shooting and grouping. As I get in better shape physically, I do wish we did more physical training. I don't know if that's the workout addiction now that I feel myself getting stronger or if we really do need to work out more. Maybe that's where the phrase "Relaxin' Jackson" comes from. As long as you try and put forth maximum efforts in your training, you won't get fucked with. It's funny because people try to run and hide and quiver at the thought of getting smoked. I enjoy it. All it is is a workout, and that's one of the reasons I joined: to get in better shape.

I had to take a stance today to get some action/results in this fire guard dilemma we are having between the two bays in building one. Remember when we got in trouble and our fire guard duty was changed from two-man shifts to four-man shifts? Well, we were never told when we would go back to two-man shifts again. Some of the guys in the first bay were talking with some of the guys in the second bay. We found out those guys only did four-man shifts for like a week. We told my bay leader (another soldier) what happened, and he acted like he was mad, but he didn't do anything about it. He didn't say anything to the drill instructor, which is the reason we told him to start with. That is the point of having a bay leader; they report back to the drill instructors about issues going on in the bay.

We all would repeatedly ask him over the weeks, "When are you going to ask about fireguard?" He would always give us a lame excuse about why he shouldn't, couldn't, or wouldn't ask. Today I just got fed up with it. We are all tired, yet the bay leader is too scared to say anything. So tonight, after hydration formation (where we form up and the instructors make us drink a canteen of water to make sure no one is dehydrated from the activities during the day), I approached the drill instructor myself. Turns out, he forgot all about us even being on four-man guard duty. He reduced it immediately. Ain't this a bitch. We could've been off this bullshit, but we have a coward as a bay leader. Once again, Lew had to save the day.

I walked back into the bay with a few battle buddies who were standing with me when I approached the drill sergeant. Announced to everyone the good news, and they all celebrated and jumped for joy! When the bay leader came back in the bay, I went to let him know the updated status of the fireguard shifts, and he was like, "I know I heard. I just wish you wouldn't have gone over my head." I spazzed out on that dude! "Mutherfucker, what you mean over your head? Bitch first off, I outrank you in the real army, don't get it twisted, you are a private, and I am a specialist, know your fucking place!" I screamed. "If you weren't acting like such a bitch, I wouldn't have had to ask, cocksucker." I continued unleashing my beast of frustrations on him. "It's either get it done or not get it done. Anything else is an excuse. You ain't get it done." Everyone was like, "Damn Tuck." He may be mad at me going forward, but I could care less. In order to make an omelet, you have to crack some eggs. Now his yolk is all over the floor.

Fuck it. Keep it real is my motto. Then I hear this other guy whisper all hoe-like, "That's why I don't even argue with Tucker." I said, "And that's the smartest thing I have ever heard you say. Keep it up, and you might go places." Enough drama for the day. I'll admit. I may have gone a little hard, but hey, I don't scratch my head unless it itches, and I don't dance unless I hear music. Ok, holler back tomorrow.

1/9/10

Today was okay, I guess. We went back to the e-range for weapons training, and to be honest, the devices are cool, but they are overrated in my opinion. There's nothing like the real deal to practice with. I just feel like I'm playing a video game (because I am). If you want to learn how to drive a car, you don't play Need for Speed, you get in a real car. My bay leader came to apologize to me today about the argument we had yesterday. I was big enough to admit I could've handled it a bit differently as well (I'm not 100% asshole). I didn't apologize for what I said, just how I said it. I indeed meant what I said.

Tomorrow is Sunday, so I don't suspect there will be much going on. On Sundays, I try to use my time and decompress as much as I can. Try to empty the tank from last week to get ready for the next week. I spent most of my time this evening reminiscing and writing letters. This is one of those days where I feel like I'm almost incarcerated, but just with no guilt about being here. I wish there was a better way mentally I could have prepared for the distance from everyone and everything I've known. Some things you just don't know until you go through them. Some things you just don't know to ask. Anyway, there's not much left to say for today. Signing off until tomorrow.

1/10/10

Today was a fairly routine day. It was ok, not too bad. I had a wonderful breakfast. After breakfast, we came back to clean the barracks and weapons. The normal routine. As we did all that, of course, as soldiers, we would shoot the shit a little bit, laughing, joking, talking about what drill sergeants we thought were assholes and who was cool, what other battle buddies we thought were going to make good soldiers. Oddly, we never talked about home that much. We didn't talk about families and where we were from. It was more about each other. We were trying to get to know each other. Hell, we were all together 24/7. We spent more time together than we would have with families. We were responsible for each other 24/7.

Yep, everything was good up until the very end of the day. Then the bullshit happened. Saturdays are laundry turn-in days. It was my understanding that laundry turn-in was optional, meaning not mandatory. Anyway, this dickhead drill sergeant writes me up for a counseling statement (minor military training disciplinary infraction). I've never been written up for anything, and he pulls this dumb shit. These drill sergeants need to all get on the same page because none of them knows what the other is doing. That ruined my damn day. Not to mention I just found out I have fire guard duty at like 03:00 and wake up is at 05:00. On top of that, I had to write this 500-word essay on how to follow orders and turn it in at 04:30. These motherfuckers don't know, I'm the king of essays. So, needless to say, there was no need to try and go back to sleep for 20 or 30 minutes, so my day tomorrow starts at 03:00. Luckily, we go to the gun range, so at least tomorrow shouldn't be boring. Taking my ass to bed now, 03:00 will be here before I know it.

01/11/2010

Pretty cool day it was. I was able to put aside last night's bullshit and focus on the new day. We went to the qualifying range today and got to shoot at the pop-up targets. This range was legit. So far, it's the best range we have been to. This range is an outdoor range that had targets set up at 50, 100, 200, 250, and 300 yards. Targets pop ups were random, and multiple targets popped up at once, giving you the choice to pick the target you want to shoot. Today wasn't mandatory to qualify when shooting, but it looks good if you can. We were there to practice, but if you qualified, then they counted the round as a qualifying round. Tomorrow it will count, so it's best to shoot as much as you can today. I didn't qualify today, but I'm confident I will tomorrow. The days now are consistently flying by now. Word was put out that Wednesday will be the final day for weapons qualification, so as of tomorrow, the heat is on. Stay tuned.

CHAPTER 17
WHITE PHASE IS UPON US

1 /12/10

Man, today was awesome! Amazing! By far the best day I've had in training. I've had a few great days, probably some I thought wouldn't get better than. Today was like the epitome of why I joined the Army. It was picture-perfect. I woke up and I wasn't tired. Felt well rested. I got outside and it wasn't freezing cold, and the sun was up and out in full. As soon as we formed this morning, we got the best news of the day. We had officially been given the news we would start the day of white phase! We had successfully transitioned. So, this means we would go to the dining hall as white phase trainees and not red phase trainees. Stoked we were. Everyone perked up then. Whoever was still sleepy woke up at that point.

White phase is the meat and potatoes of basic training. All the pictures you see and commercials with red teams and blue teams and all the madness and war activities are all white phase. White phase signifies growth. Drill instructors trust you a little more and, at the same time, expect more from you. By the time white phase rolls around, civilian mindsets should be transformed into complete military mindset. At this point, it's a way of life. Most importantly, white phase is the last phase of training where we are still learning. Blue phase is all about graduation and transitioning to the next phase of your army career.

After we ate, we headed to my favorite place, the shooting range. We went back to the qualifying range today and your boy QUALIFIED! So you know you can't tell me anything. The rest of the day was a breeze for me. I did get yelled at, however, for looking through the MREs versus grabbing and going to. I didn't care, though. I don't eat pork or beef, so I be damned If I get stuck with a stew chow or some other bullshit I don't eat and be hungry the rest of the day.

Tomorrow is technically the official qualifying day, but the drill sergeants said that if we did well today, then we didn't have to take the qualifier tomorrow. I passed today; I hit 26/40 targets. Even though I passed, I'm still going to shoot tomorrow to see if I can get a better score. I'm trying to get at least a 32/40. I believe that qualifies as a sharpshooter. Sharpshooter is right under the eagle eye (eagle eye is the best of the best). If you shoot the eagle eye, you might get an invite to sniper school. Ok, that's about it for today. I need to get my mind right for tomorrow.

1/13/10

As I said yesterday, today was the big qualifying day, and of course, I qualified! Now it's pretty much downhill from here. I think we have a few more trainings to do and classes to take, but that's it. Then we start preparing for graduation ceremonies. I can't believe how fast it's all going now. A lot of the things we do on a daily basis are second nature now, and I am even starting to notice how we are governing ourselves lately. The mean green machine is starting to become finely tuned around these parts.

I got a few letters today, but honestly, now I'm over letters; if they come, they come. I'm to the point where if you haven't written by now, you probably won't. I'm more focused on graduation and where I will be going for A.I.T (Advanced Individual Training). A.I.T is where you learn the job you signed up to do. I signed up to be a tank mechanic. I had never really seen a real tank up close and personal before, other than a museum, so I couldn't wait. I'm still enjoying basic training; it's just at this point, nothing surprises me. I'm used to the yelling, I'm used to the physical discomfort of the training, and I'm used to the discomfort of being out in the winter elements. In my experience, if you keep thinking you can't get passed something, then you won't get past it. Lights out is upon us, so let's cut this here and pick up tomorrow. Nothing else really to talk about.

1/14/10

Today was pretty routine. Not much going on. We had a surprise bay inspection, and to no surprise, our bay got tossed inside out.

The Inspection today apparently was regarding unauthorized items that were found in other bays, so I guess the Instructors said they wanted to check everyone then. All my stuff was good to go, so I helped clean the bay and some of my other battles fix their stuff. It took us about three and a half hours to clean up what the drill instructors messed up in like 10 minutes. To make things worse, while the instructors trashed the bay, they made us stay in the front leaning rest position (starting push-up position) while they trashed the bunks and bay. The more things like this happen, the more it makes me think about getting the hell out of here.

1/15/10

Today started off fairly boring. We went to the electronic range today, and my session was over by like 11:00, so I just sat around a lot. Then the day got a bit more interesting. Not because of activities, but because of dumbasses. We went to dinner chow and some assholes decided they wanted to talk in the chow line. One of our drill sergeants (the fine one all us guys stare at) hears the chatter coming from that direction and asked who it was talking to. Since no one had the balls to speak up, she made us all write 100 times, "I will not talk in formation" (pretty lame I know). The entire time she was talking, I was thinking, "that ain't shit." I wrote the little phrases in like 5 minutes.

Moving along, so we get in the DEFAC to eat, and one of the least favorable drill sergeants gives us 1 minute to eat. Everyone else was pissed about it, but that's the kind of asshole he is. By now, I know to expect the unexpected. I paid no attention and just made sure I ate the most important things on my plate. As soon as he said, "Stack 'em." I played a psychological game with myself. "Good, I'm done anyway, that was a long time," I thought while everyone else huffed and puffed. Everyone else was still saying how hungry they were, and I was telling myself how full I was. Nothing they do will I allow to phase me anymore. I know this will only last a few more weeks and then it's over. "Fuck it," is what I told myself. "I ain't doing shit else anyway and I don't have anywhere else to be." This is how you have to mentally prepare yourself for the head games they play in basic training. If you don't find little ways to trick yourself out of the hell you go through, you may crack.

Everything, literally everything, in basic training is a test. A test of discipline, strength physically and mentally, courage, endurance, patience, and emotions. I mean you name it, and it's a test. The key to it all is, when things get tough, you must maintain your focus and keep your emotions in check. Emotions have no place in training. When you let emotions guide your decisions, you will probably make the wrong choice.

Funny story time: this one soldier went AWOL tonight right after final formation at about 21:00. A few of us heard him say he was going to leave but no one believed him. I mean, I had heard stories of people running but I never really thought anyone would actually do it. You get caught and you are getting detained on the spot. Going AWOL is just bad business all around. As soon as formation let out and the drill sergeants started to head towards their quarters, the soldier took off. Headed towards the tree line. As I watched him dart off, I tapped one of my battle buddies and pointed to him, laughing. All I could think was, "Now where the hell is he going to go? He doesn't even know how to get off base". Fucking idiot! I tell ya, I have seen some funny, stupid, and crazy shit while I've been here at Fort Jackson. I swear they should make this shit a T.V. reality show (call it The Barracks, maybe this book can help me write the pilot episode to push).

Side note: I hurt my knee today, banged it pretty good, but I can't remember how. I felt like a football player again. There's always something sore or ailing, a cut or scrape somewhere, but you just push through and get the job done. We have this obstacle course tomorrow, so I hope this little setback doesn't slow me down much.

Today was fun as fuck! We did what's known as the "Confidence" course today. The course was about 6 hours long, not including lunch, and the intensity level was fairly high depending on your physicality level. We climbed ropes and ladders, dangled from 3 and 4 story towers, tumbled over logs, the whole 9 yards. The only thing I can think of to compare it to would be like an ironman competition to some extent. My knee was bothering me a little bit, but not enough to stop me from enjoying the day. Plus, I think my adrenaline was pumping so much I didn't notice it. I don't know if anyone reading this has ever played organized sports or intense playground ball, but if so, the intensity was to that level. Pickup game 3, best out of 5, going to 15, and it's game point - that level of intensity.

I did things I never thought I was capable of. There were times when we were doing team activities and we would yell and scream at each other and get to arguing, but that was all in fun and competition. We mainly yelled at the ones who acted so scary all the time, never wanting to face any fear, scared to do some of the obstacles. I can understand some of the anxieties of facing the fear, but the thing people were failing to remember was: it's a confidence course, so you have to do everything. That's the entire purpose of going through the course is to build up that confidence in yourself and to build the trust and confidence in your teammates. When Uncle Sam says you're doing something, it's not really a question or a meeting about it to see how you feel. You do as you are instructed.

I almost smacked the shit out of someone again today. I'll admit I was pestering him. I gave him a nickname (Peter Pan) he didn't like and kept calling him by it. Everyone else thought it was hilarious. That was pretty much the entire day. Tomorrow is Sunday, so we should have a pretty easy day. I believe we start a different weapons training next week, so that should be a blast. These weapons trainings are like playing video games, only with real weapons. These trainings make you forget about the things you miss back in the real world for the most part. I just wish we got more phone privileges. I understand why we don't. We have more things higher on the priority list than shooting the shit with friends and family. Hear me and hear me good when I say this. Protecting the country takes a back seat to no one, nothing, and no holiday. Enough chattering for the night. Let's hope I get some good sleep.

1/17/10

Today was really chill. Hell, I even got to sneak in a little nap earlier. We did the usual bay maintenance: sweeping, mopping floors, cleaning showers and toilets, police calling the perimeter around the living quarters, you know, same old, same old. I got a head start on the letters I wanted to send out (I ain't writing any more until I start to get some back, damn it). I write more letters than I receive by far (you will too). You would think people would write you more, knowing they can't talk to you on the phone. I guess not. Maybe it's that "Out of sight, out of mind," thing that kicks in. The thing is, that theory only applies to those that stay stationary. How come those out of my sight aren't out of my mind?

We thought we were going to get to use our phones today. Well, everyone else thought that. I don't believe in shit until shit happens, and shit didn't happen. Lesson to learn, people: Don't get your hopes up about anything while in training. When it happens, if it happens, enjoy it then, only in the moment. When it's gone, don't dwell on it because it's gone and damn sure don't wait on it to happen again because you will miss out on the now, waiting for a hope and a prayer.

Tomorrow, we do more weapons training so it's a given that is going to be fun. I believe the drill sergeants said later this week we will start advanced combative training. All this J.I. Joe shit is really making me feel like a badass. I'm about to start telling people to just call me Jason Bourne out, this bitch. Anyway, we found out our graded PT test will be on Tuesday, so my knee better be better by then. Anyone who doesn't pass is getting recycled and will have to start basic training from day 1. Fuck that shit!

Today was one of those day I missed home. As of now, Monica is the only one who writes me on a consistent basis, and I appreciate that more than I think she knows. Basically, it makes you think about things a lot and take a step back to get a better perspective on things. It will make you appreciate little shit much more. Just earlier today, me and another guy were saying, if only we could have a Dr. Pepper and a phone call, things would be much better. Most people have a soda for lunch and think nothing of it. Most people stop by a fast-food spot after work and think nothing of it. Here, in no man's land, we think that shit is heaven-like. Okay, enough for today. Tales from Army-Wood (get it, like Hollywood, but arm…never mind) will continue tomorrow.

1/18/10

Ugh, today was so long. I didn't think today would ever end. Part of the day was boring as hell, and part of the day was cool. Part of the day I was sleepy, and part of the day I was aggravated. Maybe I was aggravated because I was sleepy. We did more close combat training today along with weapons maintenance. I swear I cleaned my weapon about 4 or 5 times today. No phone calls again today. We have heard from soldiers in all other companies, and everyone else but us has had opportunities to make calls. I know I would love to hear a few of my people's voices, but it's whatever. I can't stress over that. A lot of soldiers' spirits are starting to get down again, I think, just due to all the rigorous training and the lack of sleep. Thankfully, my spirits are good, and I feel good physically. When I no longer feel I'm in this mind state, then I'll start to worry.

We didn't get mail today because of the MLK holiday. I'm starting to get addicted to mail call. I think it may be making me lose focus a little bit. For anyone who is reading this and is thinking of joining the armed forces, please do not rely on mail. Yes, it does help get through hard days, and yes, you will want to know what all is going on back home. Mail is distracting. Worry about what's going on at home when you go back home. The way I'm going to look at the mail situation going forward is like this: I'll write and let people know I'm doing ok, but I won't expect any in return. These last few weeks, I'm going to kick it into overdrive with the fitness, dieting, and self-discipline. I need to be at the top of my shit come A.I.T time.

1/19/10

Well, today pissed me off in several ways, let me count them. First, breakfast was some bullshit (you know how I am about my wake-up grub). That threw my entire day off. Second, the day was long as fuck! I thought today would never end. Wake-up was at 04:30 for the physical training test (I passed, but I'll get back to that later). Besides the day being so long, the fact that we have so many kids fucking bitching all the time didn't make it any better. All of them bitching about shit that isn't going to change. That shit blows my mind. After the PT test, we hit the range all day. When I say all day, I mean all day from 08:30 until 21:00 (9:00 p.m.). I thought we would never leave.

In case I haven't broken down how the shooting range works, let me break it down for you. Yes, shooting is fun; not too many things better to do than go to the range. Although shooting is fun, you're not shooting all day long; 60 to 70% of the time, you are standing or sitting around watching and waiting to shoot. Today we didn't even start shooting until about an hour after lunch! Mind you, we got here after breakfast. What the fuck is that all about? We could have just stayed at the barracks for this shit.

What made up for all the waiting around earlier today was the night fire session. That was intense. We got to use night vision goggles and tracer rounds. For those who don't know what a tracer round is, a tracer round of ammunition has a flammable painted tip that burns once the round is fired. The tip lights up and is used as a reference point for round accuracy and location. It keeps the shooter focused on the target point. You can literally see the round light up and fly until it hits a target. We loaded our magazines so that every third round was a tracer round. This is done to help with consistency. I see why the military loves fucking shit up. We have immaculate weaponry.

The night vision goggles were pretty cool. I would think, in Today's age with the advancement of technology, you would think they wouldn't be as bulky as they are, but maybe there will be some modifications coming soon. When I say it was pitch black dark, I mean "can't see a hand in front of my face," dark, with no sense of sight whatsoever. We put those goggles on, and everything was crystal clear. The vision coloring was a green tent with a black and white feel, but the pixels were amazing. I could distinctly see leaves and tree branches on trees as if it were daytime. It truly is a great piece of technology.

The night experience truly made up for my feelings earlier during the day. Ok, well let's wrap this up for today. I still have fireguard duty tonight, and tomorrow we are scheduled for a 9-mile road march. The good thing is my boots are comfortable. I can't stress enough. Success in the military lies in the care you take of your feet. Can't do anything without them.

CHAPTER 18
TRAINING SOMETHING FIERCE

1 /20/10

Today was amazing! Absolutely! I was well rested waking up this morning. We did a 12.5 mile road march today that I thought was awesome. I'm sure some people would disagree with me and probably thought it was hell. The road march was done in full combat gear or, as we say, "full battle rattle." Full gear includes helmet, rifle, pullet proof plates and vest, canteen, rucksack (backpack about 40 pounds filled with a change of gear, e-tool (a small collapsible shovel), and other necessities. It was probably about 85 pounds of additional weight on us we carried for the march. We had two major hills during the march we had to endure, and they were steep indeed. Steep enough where you can lean forward and touch the ground. This was the best workout we have done by far since we got here. It took about four and a half hours to complete (05:50–09:40 a.m.) Then we had U.S. weapons training.

U.S. weapons training, this is what everyone waits for and wants to do in basic training. No, no. These weapons make the rifles look like NERF pop guns. We got to shoot the M249, M240, the A24 rocket launcher, and the holy grail of badasses, the 50-caliber machine gun. We also got to toss live grenades and fire several other weapons. Now, firing the weapons was cool, but what made it awesome, was the range setup. The range first was huge. I'm talking, 600– 700 yards deep and about 400 yards wide. It was staged with buses and cars and bikes and buildings. The range was set up like a small town or at least a few blocks in a small town. They set the range up this way so we can see the impact and the damage that these weapons do. I felt like Bruce Willis in all 3 Die Hard movies the way we were firing off. I mean, belts and belts of ammunition. I think I may have shot literally a few thousand rounds of ammunition personally. You would be surprised how fast you can fire off a 50-round clip of ammunition. I think my favorite was the M240 machine gun. It fired so smooth, and the recoil was easy to handle. Some of those weapons were so powerful they hurt to fire.

Today was fun, but it flew by so quickly. To top the day off, I got mail! Monica sent me a care package, which was the best, along with other mail from friends. The mail I got today will carry me emotionally through the rest of training. I can't wait to read my letters. I think I'll spread the reading out over a few days to give me something to look forward to before lights out. I was tempted to read them all tonight, but I wanted to make sure I wrote in my journal before I went to sleep. I wonder what tomorrow will bring. I hope another great adventure. I was talking to my favorite drill instructor today, and she was telling me as far as training, we are basically done after U.S. weapons and from there we will go to blue phase. I can't wait. Blue phase is the part I have been waiting for. This is the part we have endured so much pain and struggle and bullshit to get to. No way I'm backing down now. Less than a month to go. I amaze myself every day. Even though I knew I could do it and I knew I would do it. It's still wonderful to see myself actually accomplishing it.

1/21/10

Today was ok, which is really an overstatement. I really didn't do anything special. We went to the range to practice cover shooting, which was boring. It was boring mainly because, first, it was bad weather. It was cold, rainy, and muddy. I could deal with the elements if I was active the whole time, but we only got to go through 1 crate a piece, which is about 320 rounds or so. I guess I have been spoiled by the unlimited rounds of ammunition we have had access to up until this point. I shot early, so I pretty much stayed in the bleachers all day like a spectator.

During a break, I guess the drill sergeants got wind that a few soldiers were doing impressions of drill sergeants, so they asked us to do some impressions. I thought it was a setup, but they enjoyed it. We all had good laughs, which was needed. It helped lighten the seriousness and the tension with everyone. I did a few impressions of some of the instructors, and everyone got a kick out of it. Even the drill sergeants were laughing, which was good. I know this has to be hard for them too, and I also know we don't see all the things they go through or understand their stress levels. As the saying goes, "The grass ain't always greener on the other side." That's not the first time I had everyone laughing (maybe I am a funny guy).

Tomorrow, we go get fitted for our class A uniforms. That's the uniform that looks like a suit, that's the formal attire. I believe we graduate in those. It's pretty cool because all of those are tailor-made. So, my uniform will be custom-made to fit me and only me. I would say it's free, but I have learned nothing is free in the mean green machine. I haven't heard from my sisters in a while. Maybe they just don't like writing letters. I've only gotten one letter apiece from each of them in the seven and a half weeks I have been here. I'm not sure how I feel about that. Nevertheless, I'm here to train, not read letters.

1/22/10

Pretty good day, I must say. It went by fast as well. We went back to the 120th reception battalion. That's where we first arrived when we got to Fort Jackson. Here, we got our class A uniforms, and I must admit, they are sharp. Everything is starting to sink in now that graduation is nearing. At first, I didn't like the class A uniforms (probably because I didn't have one yet). I wish we were graduating in them. That's pretty much all we did all day. Trying to fit 243 soldiers for uniforms can take a while.

I must admit, it was a bit nostalgic going back to reception. Seeing the newbies there made me feel like it was so long ago. I can also see the drastic improvement or change in myself as well as my battle buddies. The metamorphosis from civilian to soldier. There were a few soldiers that stopped me from being inquisitive and asked what was in store for them. It's funny because I know exactly how they feel. I know exactly what they are thinking and how nervous they are. I could see it in their eyes. I gave honest opinions as well as what I thought was pretty good advice. I just hope they take my advice.

Word on the street is we go to blue phase next week, around Wednesday or Thursday. That's when you know it's a wrap. Tomorrow, we have more hand-to-hand combative training. I love combative training. My drill sergeant teaches that class, and he is a beast. Definitely not the guy to fuck with. The thing is, he doesn't even look like he's a problem. If you saw him on the street, you would think, "Oh, I can take this guy," wrong answer. This dude is fearless and relentless. Okay, well, time to hit the hey, you know the drill, you know how it goes. Same time tomorrow, hopefully with a good adventure to tell.

1/23/10

Today was cool. We got up and went for a 2-mile run at a nice and steady pace. Personally, I thought it was too slow a pace. I like to be pushed; anything other than that, to me, is a waste of time. After the run, we had combative training again. Once combative training was over, we went to throw the M67 grenades. This was another practice session for the next live grenade session. We go get haircuts tomorrow, then to the post exchange to grab some necessary toiletries.

We have this thing called "Victory Anvil," on Monday for three days. From my understanding, it's a field training exercise. This is supposed to be a prerequisite to what's called, "Victory Hammer," which is a six day field exercise training, like a rite of passage before graduation. We are supposed to learn and apply tactical bounding techniques in two-man teams as well as some other things. I forgot the rest they say we will be doing, guess I'll write about that after it happens. In a way, I'm excited about this camping trip, well, at least that's what I'm calling it. I don't know what else to call it. I know we are not roasting marshmallows and singing songs or no shit like that. I just don't know how else to describe it.

With that being said, I'm also kind of nervous about it because I don't know what to expect. On top of that, I'm sick of eating MREs. On top of those things, it's also cold. Plus, from my understanding, you don't get mail while out in the field. I love mail. You know, I'm just going to make the best of it. The last thing I need to do is go out there with a fucked up attitude and make things worse. The quickest way out is to move forward, so that's what I'm going to do. Toughen up, man up, and get it done.

Oh shit, news alert before I forget. Some of the drill instructors have started notifying soldiers of who's in danger of getting restarted back to white phase! I said WHITE phase! Oh, hell no! As of now, I haven't heard an exact number regarding how many people have been notified, but I hear it's somewhere between 17 and 21 so far. Out of like 64 people, that's huge! That's like a 3rd of the platoon. There's no way I could do this shit again from the top. You mean start over like, all we did was practice this whole time? No sir, not me, not this guy, not this time. I think I'd have to go AWOL. Yeah, I said it, I'm bailing. Now I'm going to start looking around to see who has the sad faces on. Who has a look of disgust and sickness and failure on their face? Then I'll know who it was, then I'll know who I can think and say, "Yup, figures, I thought so." Just know I'm not going to be one of them, damn it!

I am good for now, but I can't lie, the amount of stress you go through physically and mentally (especially if you are not already in particularly good shape) is crazy. The wear and tear on your body takes a toll (especially on the knees). Then there is the lack of sleep plus the continuous grind of every minute of every hour of every day is just beastly! I can't stress it enough.

Now, back to this training trip. Our packing list seems like it's everything in the world that we have to take, and only two bags to bring it all in. There's going to be a lot of cramming involved. I'm glad that I listened and paid attention to the packing instructions they gave us. Hell, they even have a regulation on how to fold and tuck every clothing item so that it all fits. I'm telling you, this shit is calculated down to the tee in every scenario. Now I get there will be a lot of packing involved, but the thing that makes me mad the most is I know; I mean I know for a fact and can guarantee that after we are all packed up, The drill sergeants are going to make us dump it all out again. They do it specifically to make sure that they can check to see if everyone has everything. Then we will have to put it all back again, only this time we won't be in the bays at our bunks doing it, we will be outside on the drill pads in the cold.

1/24/10

Today was pretty good. We didn't do too much, and I was well-rested throughout the day. I was able to take a nap from around 11:00 a.m. until about 12:30 or so (pretty sweet, huh?). We spent all day packing and unpacking to pack up again and load the trucks in preparation for our field outing. We were running late or behind with everything today for some reason, so we were the last ones to chow for every meal. You don't want to be last for chow for several reasons.

Anything that can go wrong will go wrong towards the end of chow. You get the last of all the food, portions are not as generous, some food may be out so your meal isn't complete, and you're getting rushed out of the chow hall because they are trying to either clean and prep for the next meal, or clean and prep to close shop. These are those times where you have to really keep your shit together and remember to play the game. People can get a little out of character when they are exhausted and hungry.

The drill sergeants are calming down more and more now that we have so little time left. I feel like I'm starting to see the human side to most of them. Now, I'm not saying that means they are not really badasses because they are, please believe me, but I now can see them as mothers, fathers, wives, husbands, sisters, and brothers, as well as fearless leaders. From the changes I see in me so far, and from the hell I feel like I've been through to get here. I will say this: I appreciate, and respect, and admire the hell out of my drill sergeants. Anybody that doesn't or didn't feel some sort of admiration towards their sergeants didn't have good drill sergeants.

Damn, tomorrow morrow morning we head out. I'm not looking forward to eating these MREs for the next few days, but fuck it, guess it beats being hungry. On a good note, the weather hasn't been cold. I just pray it stays that way for the next few days. I'm excited, nervous, and anxious about the experience. I keep saying I'm just ready to get it over with but I'm not. I don't want to just get it over with. I want to experience it. I just don't want to be disappointed. I don't even know what I think I'm going to be disappointed about. I just know it better be good damn it!

CHAPTER 19
VICTORY FUCKING ANVIL

1 /25/10

First day of field exercises complete. The first day was cool for most of it. I don't think I can get down with this sleeping outside shit, though. Of course, dinner was some bullshit, but it's cool though. Allegedly, I'm in this so-called state-of-the-art sleeping bag, but I can't get the damn thing zipped all the way up.

We learned more maneuvering skills today. Some of the sessions were interesting, but I think I'm starting to get drained mentally. It feels like a weight was just placed on my back. The non-stop, 24 hours a day, G.I. Joe stuff is starting to get to me. I'm tired, and I think this is the first time I think I may be starting to feel "homesick." Today went by fast, but the next few weeks can't go by fast enough. At least that's how I'm feeling now. I'm hoping tomorrow will be a different story. I just pray for strength to make it through. I hope all my loved ones are praying too, because in the moment, I'm like, "fuck this shit." For now, I guess I'll seek comfort in this little ass tent until morning comes.

1/26/10

Wow! What a day, and what to say. Emotionally, today was my lowest point that I have hit during basic training. I was awakened by an uncontrollable shiver and some 5 a.m. whistle blowers. Not only was it cold outside simply because it was January, but it was freezing inside the tent too. Incoherently, I fumbled around in my tent trying to get dressed. All the while thinking, "This is some bullshit." I mean, the chill swooshed through my sheets and all of the layers of my clothing. Drill sergeants were yelling and screaming. "Let's go let's go let's move, move, move! That shit gets aggravating, especially in the cold at 5 a.m. in the morning. I'm really not loving this field exercise.

As I stood in the breakfast line, waiting to be served my chow, I started to feel really down. I started kicking around irrational thoughts in my head and could find no way to rid myself of them. Now I know in this situation, I am or can be my own worst enemy. I felt my eyes start to water and tried so hard to fight back any signs of tears from letting this bullshit get to me. Believe me when I say, this psychological mind fucking is crazy! You must stay sharp here in this place. Missing my friends, family, home, and all, I started second guessing myself. Then, I had to snap the fuck out of it. Just like that, I did. I reminded myself that we only had two more weeks after this week, and it'll all be over with.

I kept telling myself, "Look how much you've done, Lew, no turning back now!" Not to mention, we were learning some great maneuvers: how to enter and clear houses from hostiles. That shit is intense. As I reassured myself, the day did get better. Then it happened. The one thing that got me over the hump. The best letter I have received so far came. Monica wrote me. As I read the letter (all three pages), different emotions roared through me. Her words were thoughtful, encouraging, motivating, and from the root of sincerity. I could not have received this letter at a better time. She served me with the food for thought I desired, and the plate was served hot. That letter, I know, will make tomorrow easier.

I knew, or at least I thought I knew, that basic training would be hard, at least physically. I never knew mentally or emotionally it would be anywhere near this challenging. When I finish this challenge, it will definitely be placed up there right under college graduation as one of the toughest things I've done up until this point in my life. After the way the morning started, I definitely didn't think it would end the night on this good of a note.

1/27/10

Thank God we are back at the fucking barracks! I hate the field, let's just get that out of the way right now! I hate it with a passion. I hate it with every inch of hatred I can possibly have. It was cold, it was rainy, and my fingers were still numb and tingling from the weather. Rest was not the thing to look for on this exercise. I wasn't as cold last night as I was the night prior, but the night was still uncomfortable.

Today was wasted on waiting around, in my opinion. We woke up really early (05:00), packed up our shit, and just bullshit around until about 4 p.m. when we hiked to the bus to return back to the barracks. The only thing I liked was that I didn't have to eat any more MREs. We got to eat at the dining facilities. News break: remember when I said some people were getting recycled through basic training? That all happens tomorrow. The soldiers who were not excelling were given the option to restart or be chaptered out of the armed forces. A chapter out is an early release without any tarnishing of your civilian record. There is no disciplinary action, in other words. Most of them, I think, deserved it. A lot of them were faking being sick or being crazy and, just quite frankly, didn't belong in the service.

I'll admit, I would've been mad as hell if those same ones had graduated with me and got to march across that big green field with the crowd watching and cheering. I and all my other battle buddies bled, sweat, and cried together and went through pure hell. Those other fakers don't deserve the honor of being able to walk with us. Fuck those guys.

Side note: I think I'm getting sick again. In basic training, it is extremely important to keep your hands clean. We touch so much shit, and so many people touch the same things, you're bound to get sick. I spent so much time on my break trying to get better, get back here, and now I'm sick again, son of a bitch! Being sick in basic training is the worst because you still have to push hard and deal with the outdoor elements that probably contributed to your illness in the first place. For those that follow behind me in joining the service, please, for your sake, keep your hands washed. Remember, just because you think you're a sanitary person doesn't mean others are.

CHAPTER 20
ALL CLEAR SKIES

This week is speeding by, and that's perfectly ok with me. Two more weeks and Ft. Jackson can kiss my ass! As each day passes, I get more and more ready for the next phase of learning, which is advanced individual training (A.I.T). Tomorrow will be an easy day. We have what's called post clean up. Post clean-up is different units doing just that: cleaning up assigned outdoor areas, picking up trash, cutting grass in some situations, washing windows, what we call "grunt" work. I'll take it though. Yeah, it's boring, but for the most of it, it's not so physically demanding.

We got official word that we will all be shipping out to our prospective A.I.T destinations on the 20th of February. No going home for me in between. I actually don't know the next time I'll be going home, and I'm okay with that. I didn't leave to want to hurry back. I'm just ready to leave here, ready to leave this place and see something new once again. As soon as I can, I'm going to start sending my sister some money. She wrote me, and the letter had a pretty stressful tone to it. I guess everyone is dealing with issues in some form daily. Oh, word on the street is we move to blue phase on Friday! At this point, who cares about colors or phases? I just care about the ship out date. Call it whatever color you want. Well, lights out for me. 04:00 will be here before I know it.

1/28/10

Today was more was really chill, even more chill than Sundays. We did have post clean up today, but that was a joke. We cleaned up for about two hours and then chilled extra hard for the rest of the day. We ate lunch at the lake, which was rather soothing, I must say. Shit, I can do this every day until it's time to go. We are supposed to go to blue phase tomorrow. Now that's what I want to see. End of the road jack. We have grenade class tomorrow, so I'm ready for that. That should definitely be interesting. A few of the females have been whispering about being scared. Fuck that. I'm trying to be "Rambo" out here.

As the days pass by, drill instructors are definitely laying off more. I just wished we had more time for chow; that's the only thing that hasn't changed, that and sleep. I'm just trying to take it day by day. Seems like the less I think about it, the faster time passes by. Our final and graded physical training test is next week, and this one is for all the marbles. This is the one that goes on your record that will stay with your permanent files. I'm more anxious about taking that test than anything else. Victory Forge, the weeklong exercise is approaching, and I'm not even mad about it. Once that is over, basic training is over.

1/29/10

Well, today was kind of disappointing. Don't get me wrong, everything went according to plan, it just wasn't as exciting as I envisioned it being. We did get to throw a few rounds of live grenades, and that was awesome. It was exactly what they said it would be. It just wasn't as fun as firing the .50 caliber weapons or some of the other weapons we got to test out. I think they just scheduled the main event before the last show. U.S. weapons training was the big kaboom. In my opinion, that training should have been last. It's like having the playoffs and then the regular season starting.

We finished up around 14:00 and bussed back to the barrack. Once we were back at the barracks, we were instructed to clean weapons (busy work). While some were doing weapons maintenance, others were taken to turn in class A uniforms for cleaning. We didn't go to blue phase today. I really didn't expect to, considering the final physical training test isn't until Monday. That test will make or break a lot of people. I actually feel bad for the ones that have been trying to pass but just haven't been making it. Then, there are some that deserve to fail. The Army doesn't hand out free rides (or meals for that matter); you earn your keep, that's for certain. My theory is, "If you can't find a way, then make a way." End of the day, you either got it done, or you didn't. Anything else of the day is an excuse, valid or not. So, I say, let there be no excuses.

1/30/10

Today was cold as hell! I mean freezing cold, like 14 degrees. Because of the temperature, we didn't do too much outside. We learned how to tie some bullshit ass knots in our FLC vest to hold our water canteens and chilled. Oh, I got my graduation plaques back today that I ordered, which seems like forever ago. They look good. The best part about today is that we finally got to use our phones! Hallelujah! That was so much needed. I didn't realize how much I needed to hear familiar voices. We only got to use the phones for 10 minutes, but hey, that's better than nothing. I can assure you any phone time was greatly appreciated. Some of the other battles were emotional when they were talking to their loved ones. Some cried after they hung up the phones. Overall, it was just a great surprise for us and our families and friends.

Crazy story time. So, we were all formed up, waiting to go to the last chow of the day. We were ready to step off and start the march when one soldier started seizing. Dropped to the ground and started convulsing on the spot. A fucking seizure! Can you believe this shit? Everyone is screaming for the drill sergeant's aid. Ambulances came, military police came, it was a scene. Not to sound insensitive, but of course, we were late for chow. Come to find out, the guy was faking it the entire damn time. Who does that shit? Just out of nowhere, just fake a seizure. That's fucking nuts. I'm telling you, you can't make this shit up. People do some crazy shit to try and get out of the service or to get attention. Don't fake a serious medical condition. Now that I think of it, this isn't the first time the guy did this. Now I'm thinking he may have faked the first one too.

1/31/10

Today was relaxed as well. For some reason lately, I always have to wake up like an hour before the wake-up call to go pee. That is so irritating. Then it's hard to get back to sleep, and by the time I do, it's time to get up again. Anyway, today was relaxed mostly for the entire day. We formed up for our normal morning formation, went to breakfast, and came back to the barracks until lunch. After lunch, we met with the T-shirt lady to help design our graduation T-shirts (which we had to pay for). At first, I wasn't going to buy one, but then I said, "What the hell, why not?" It's funny and ironic that as much as I want and can't wait to get out of this place, I keep buying things to remind me of it. I figure I'll appreciate it later. Other than the T-shirt lady, nothing much happened. She was the highlight of the day.

Tomorrow is the big P/T day. The last physical training day of basic training. This is the one for the records. There's no way in hell I'm not passing this one. I can't even think about not passing because there is no way in hell. I'm doing this all over again from day one. I'll take the chapter out before I go through this again. Most of us are nervous, some are scared, and some are anxious. When I pass this test tomorrow, I will consider myself done!

2/1/10

Today started out great! I killed my P/T test! I got a new personal best on my run and in my sit-ups. My 2-mile run time was 14:12, down from 14:50. The atmosphere was great. We all encouraged one another. We all screamed and cheered for each other like it was the Olympics or something. That shit works, people do feed off other positive vibes. Coming around those curves running, you love hearing people cheer for you by name, hitting those push-ups and sit-ups, you love seeing people grind it out work through the pain to achieve goals. I was inspired. I was done pretty early, but I hung around the track and field to support my battle buddies. Plus, there was nothing going on in the barracks and everyone else was out here. It was fun. I enjoyed the comradery. Watching other soldiers beat their personal best and hit their personal goals was gratifying as well. We could all see the work paying off.

CHAPTER 21

GETTIN' SHOT AT

fter the P/T test, we headed to lunch and got some rest in preparation for the night fire training we had tonight. Night fire infiltration course, it's called officially. Night fire was pretty cool. First and foremost, it was with live fire rounds. That scared the shit out of me. Of course, some people didn't want to do it and were scared. I can understand the fear because, well, they're shooting live ammunition at you. They gave us the safety briefing regarding keeping our heads down, staying low on the ground, and staying calm. This exercise was like what you would see in the movies. Crawling through mud, crawling under barbed wire, tracer round bullets flying overhead. It was the real deal.

As we filed through the lines to go through the course, it seemed like it was short, maybe about 15-20 minutes a session as we watched as spectators. It looked exciting. It was entertaining to watch. You could hear people screaming; some people froze up. One guy got tackled by the drill instructors for trying to get up and run. They had to cease fire and all. They ceased fire just in time too. Right as the soldier was about to crack under pressure, they called the cease fire. He got up and started running, tripping over people and yelling, up until he got bulldozed by the drill sergeant, then he came back to his senses. They let him go get a sip of water and then put him back in the line to do it over again. They told him if he couldn't complete the course he would not graduate and would either get kicked out or recycled.

As my time approached for my cycle to go through, I'll admit I was nervous. Hell, hell, I'm always nervous when it comes to drills or things I never did before, and that's natural. I just wasn't letting that control the fact that I wanted to do the drill. Everything else I have done, I have gone headfirst, so that's what I did. I took a deep breath, waited for the signal, and put my face in the dirt. Low crawling the entire way, it was probably about 300 yards, but man, it felt like 3 miles. I thought the drill would never end. It looked so much easier, and the wire looked so much higher off the ground than it was. I felt like the barbed wire was right in my face, like if I moved the wrong way, I'd get cut.

You not only could hear the bullets whizzing by up above, but you could see the tracer rounds flying by too. I thought that was great training to include the tracer rounds. You can really see how fast those bullets travel. The amount of distance they cover in a second is unbelievable. I didn't have time to look around at people because, as soon as we got the green light to start, there was another group that started about a minute after us so we had to keep moving or we would slow up the line. You don't want to be the one that slows up the line under fire. The rounds don't stop unless there is a cease fire, and you don't want to be the one that causes a cease fire. I was tired, I was chilly, and I was wet. Even though I felt all of these strains of the training, I thought it was still fun!

Once my session was over, I headed back to the holding area and sat at the top of the bleachers so I could continue to watch everyone complete the cycles. The chill turned to cold, and eventually, the sleepiness started to creep up. Some of the drills decided it was time to start bussing some of the soldiers back to the barracks that were done with training so we could start cleaning the sleeping quarters and training gear. I don't know why they don't always do that. I think it would be more efficient. Once I returned to the barracks, I hit the showers. I knew everyone wasn't back yet, so I had plenty of time to shower. I rinsed my gear off as well to speed up the process. We all shower in a central area, with no individual shower stalls, and I was just as dirty as my equipment was, so as I washed and the filth left my body, it left my equipment as well. Just as I finished, the next wave of soldiers was coming back. By 23:30 everyone had returned, and formation was at 1200. The ones who got back first started fire guard duties first, being that they had the most time off. My wave was in charge of cleaning, and the last wave would take over fireguard duties once the first wave was done.

I have CQ duty again tonight. This is the 3rd night in a row that I have had CQ duty. I wish my bay leader knew what he was doing when it came to scheduling soldiers and duties. He always lets' first bay run over him and second bay (our bay) always gets stuck with the bullshit duties and hours. On top of that, today was linen turn-in (for bed sheets), but they didn't have any fresh sheets for tonight. So, the drill instructors said to sleep in our sleeping bags. Now why the hell would I want to sleep in my sleeping bag on my bed? Not only was this recommended, but it was also mandated. We can't just sleep in our sweatpants/suits; we have to get in the bag. Hopefully, I can get some decent sleep.

2/2/10

The day was good, but the weather was horrible. A cold, cloudy, and rainy day it was. What made it worse was we had training outside all day, and I do mean every single minute we were doing something, it was outside. We did what's called Omaha training today with live fire. Omaha is where we practiced 2-man bounding tactics. The training was exciting, but short-lived. We only got to run the course twice due to the amount of people who had to cycle through and the weather. It was just as good from an excitement standpoint as night training was, just a short experience.

Tomorrow, we have this thing called "fit to win." "Fit to win," is a team obstacle course. We were supposed to have done it in like week two or three of basic training, but our session got rained out, so this is our reschedule. The drill instructors say we will enjoy this, and I take them at their word. So far, all of the other courses have been exhilarating, so I have no reason to think this one won't be also.

Two good things that happened today. First, we finally got to let off our M16 and M4 weapons on full automatic bursts. Most drill sergeants don't like burst mode because they think it's inaccurate. I think it's very accurate within about 75 meters or so. The second best thing that happened was the day went pretty smoothly. Smooth days are fast days, and fast days are the best days. Smooth means no drama, no drill instructors spazzing out, no thousand dumb ass questions from soldiers, no delays to or in the chow hall, and no unnecessary stress. Most of all, the buses came on time! This is big because typically, buses are anywhere from 30 minutes to 2 HOURS late! How ironic. For the military to pride themselves on time, the buses are always late. I can't think of one bad thing about the day besides the weather, and that is something that can't be controlled. Let's hope the remainder of training is like this.

2/3/10

Today was laid back. We did do the "Fit to Win" challenge course, but it only took like 30 minutes. I won't lie, the course was really fun! It was just short and challenging. We went through about 15 obstacles. Once everyone cycled through, each participating platoon chose their best six candidates to form a team to compete against the other platoons for the title of the best fit platoon. My platoon won, but we didn't get shit but a pat on the back for winning. It was still fun though. After that, we just chilled and did weapon maintenance all day. We could tell the drill sergeants didn't feel like doing anything and frankly, neither did we. Seems like today everyone was like, "fuck it!"

Tomorrow there is nothing planned either. It's "Drill Sergeant's Day," whatever that is. I know we are going to the barbershop for haircuts and to the post exchange. Outside of that, I haven't heard of anything planned regarding training or exercises. Time is winding down, and everyone now is really just waiting for Saturday to go to "Victory Forge." Hopefully, it will be fun! I'll settle for at least warm. Being outside in the cold for extensive periods is definitely for the birds. The Base sent letters out to family members of soldiers letting them know to stop sending mail after the 4th of this month. Yes, that's tomorrow! We all have started the formal countdown as of yesterday. 13 days left and then we will ship out. Now, everyone's motivation is the countdown. Whenever someone feels like giving up now or gets fed up, we all just say. "13 days," and it helps instantly to shake the funk off. So that is the meat for today. Report back tomorrow.

2/4/2010

Omg Ugh! Today was so, so boring. We did absolutely NOTH-ING! From 05:30 until lunchtime, all we did was sit in the class-room and look at each other. We were supposed to be cleaning weapons, but since we just cleaned weapons yesterday, after about 30-45 of cleaning today, there really isn't anything left on the rifle to clean. We got our packing list for "Victory Forge" today, but we didn't get the allotted time to pack. I guess they say they will save that for tomorrow. Once again, we will be packing and unpacking because something will change with the list. Repacking and then unpacking again to make sure we had everything packed we were instructed to pack. We also get our platoon photos back tomorrow. Yep, things are winding down. The fat lady hasn't sung yet, but she's in the dressing room warming up. I think what I will do is buy the smallest package I can to save on cost, then take the picture to Walmart or some-where and make copies.

I can't wait to see the look on everyone's faces when they see me in my uniform. It's funny because some days, I can't even believe myself that I joined forces with the mean green machine. Lewis is an army man. I remember not that long ago, maybe a few years back, I was so anti-military I'm pretty sure I even said, "I'll NEVER join the military." Apparently, things do change. That's why there is the saying, "Never say never". I, like a lot of us, was so rebellious in my 20's. I thought I knew more than most and didn't know shit. So much has changed since then and rightfully so. Yes, I needed a job to support myself. Mostly, I just wanted to do something different. Challenge myself in ways I never would have when I was home. Ways that my friends can't help me, and my family can't help me push myself. Face some fears I didn't and did know I had.

I heard from my homeboy DJ, and he writes that shit is still the same at home. People still doing the same things, moving the same ways, thinking the same things. I don't want that. I won't have that. Today, tomorrow, next year, I always want to strive to be better than I was the day before. I strive to be smarter, wiser, stronger, faster, sharper - you name it. To be better for tomorrow, I have to get my rest tonight though. Lights out.

CHAPTER 22
THE LAST HURRAH!

2 /5/10

There are few words to describe today: packing, chilled, relaxed, and wet. All day, and I do mean all day, was spent packing, washing clothes, and more packing. Preparing for this 5-day, 4-night voyage we set out on tomorrow. We will leave the barracks, hopefully for the last time, in an effort to return as bonafide soldiers. The trip will be the culmination of everything we have endured and learned during our time here in training. This is it, the last hurrah. After this, it's all out-processing and graduation ceremony practice. I'm a little nervous about the expedition, but I'm starting to get excited. I'm better prepared this time than I was last time. It could be because I know this is the last time we have to do this. Exactly 14 days left, or as we say in the military, "13 days and a wake up".

There are mixed feelings throughout the platoon as far as who wants to go and how we all feel about it. I think everyone is just nervous for the most part. We don't know what to really expect, and we won't have the drill instructors to guide us through problem solving. We were told the instructors would actually be playing the enemies. How's that even fair? These muthafuckas are proven battle tested warriors. We got people out here who want a wet wipe every time their hand gets dirty. One thing I will say is, a lot of the females that were soft earlier on in basic training are now with the program. I don't know if it's because they are just as tired of the bullshit, or if it is because they actually believe now that they can do way more than they thought they were capable of. A lot of the males have humbled themselves, and I think we realize we can't do everything alone and save everyone by ourselves.

This shit really does break you down and rebuild you. Physically, mentally, and emotionally it's all draining. It's all challenging, frustrating, and demanding. I think it's really a look in the mirror. A long look at what you are about, what limits you placed on yourself for no reason. Basic training is a purge. A purge of all weaknesses and self-doubt. This field exercise is a measuring stick for all involved. We all want to prove ourselves worthy. Everyone wants to be a good soldier, well, most of us. I just think in life everyone goes into a new job wanting to be good at it. But in the military, you really want to be good at it because you can easily get labeled as someone who is lazy to say it politely.

Wake up for tomorrow is 05:00, which will be here before I know it. I'm putting my warrior face on for the next few days (Saturday-Wednesday). I mean, if I must be out here, I do want to try and have some fun. Plus, it's been hyped up so much, I want to at least have some faith that it will live up to expectations. Oh, there was one more thing that happened today that further let me know we are almost done. We got our platoon pictures back. With this no facial hair thing, I look like a freaking kid. My face hadn't been that naked since I started growing facial hair. I purchased a few pictures for nostalgic purposes anyway. I'm not a big fan of how they placed the United States flag in the background; it's kind of cheesy but it'll do. Lights out now, next wake up, it's game time.

2/6/10

Today was the first day of Victory Forge. Not the best of days, but not the worst of days. I think the first day of Victory Hammer (the last field event) was worse. We didn't do too much today. We spent the first half of the day unpacking, then ate lunch. After lunch, we had a team bonding exercise but that was about it. Dinner was hot A's, I swear, I hate hot A meals. Hot A meals are hot meals transported from the main base out to the field units in warmers. It's not enough food and they always run out of something. If your platoon isn't one of the first 3 or 4 platoons to go through the chow line, chances are they will be out of something to complete the meal.

After dinner, we didn't really do too much except try to hide from the cold. So far that's not working. That's the worst thing for me, being cold. One day down, 4 to go. I will say this, the guys I'm in a tent with are getting on my last nerve already. I fucking hate teenagers now. I swear, I don't think I was like this new generation when I was growing up. They stay on some bullshit and all they talk about is bullshit. Not to mention, they are always loud as hell. It's whatever though, I have less than two weeks left with these clowns and I'm out. Ok, that's it for now. Same time, different day.

2/7/10

Today is over! Oh my God, I'm so glad. It wasn't a bad day at all. It was a good day, in fact. It was a bit on the chilly side, but not cold, and the sun was out mostly all day. We did more bounding exercises with blank fire rounds. The training was fun and fairly intense. I got to shoot the 249 squad automatic weapon, that shit is a monster. That's probably my favorite weapon I've fired so far. After we did the bounding exercise, the day was pretty much over. We marched back to the F.O.B. (forward operating base), had chow, and that was it. Today Is the Super Bowl so I think a lot of the drill instructors are leaving to go watch the game. I have money riding on the colts to beat the saints, so hopefully, that's an easy $20 in my pocket.

Everyone is ready to leave the camp site for the most part. I hear the snickering and gripes under soldiers' voices and out loud at times. There is tension growing among the soldiers and you can feel it. I think it's because we are all just tired of each other, tired of this experience. Just tired all around. We are all so excited about leaving and graduating I think there is some displaced anger and aggression. This doesn't upset me like others because I get it. Once tomorrow gets here, we will be halfway through the exercise. Lord, please help me get through this without cursing anybody out. Tomorrow is supposed to be relaxed as well.

Tomorrow will be like today again. Going over the same drills, the only difference is tomorrow we will be having paintball wars doing the simulations. That should be fun. Now you can really get shot and from what I hear, paintball hurt like hell. I did learn a lot from the exercises, so I think I'll be well prepared for tomorrow's simulation. My team is pretty good, no dumbasses. Ok, well, that's it for today. Hopefully, I'm not writing tomorrow all shot up.

2/8/10

Today felt like Groundhog's Day. It literally was the exact same thing as yesterday. It looked the same, it felt the same, and we did the same thing. This time, there was one difference: the course was much longer. We only got to do the course once, but it was fun while it lasted. When the morning started, it was cold as shit. Cold, like 16 damn degrees, then it warmed up a little. I hate the fucking mornings; that's by far the worst part of the day. Once I'm up for the day, I'm good to go. I miss the barrack bays. Sounds funny, I know. The barracks are no Taj Mahal, but at least I didn't wake up freezing. You take simple things for granted when you're out in the field. It's only when you get out in the field for a while that you realize what the simple things mean to you.

The thing that's getting to me the most, outside of the cold when we wake up, are these damn youngsters. Singing stupid shit all the time, talking stupid shit all the time. All of them pretending to be so hardcore and none of them are. I can tell they all chucked full of shit! For the most part, the kids that are in my unit, I can tell, were sheltered but personified being hardcore. I hate that shit! Punkass white boys and stupid little boys of color black and brown. Now, don't get me wrong, I'm not racist, I just call it how I see it. Ok, enough of the tangent for me tonight. Let me get some rest.

2/9/10

Today was just ok. It rained all day but wasn't as cold, though, as yesterday and the previous days. The cold would've been a killer, I know. Breakfast was cool though. By now, you guys should know how I feel about my breakfast meal. I guess they decided to actually give us some good portions today. We got six sausage links today, a good portion of grits, a good portion of scrambled eggs versus a damn tablespoon full, and two pancakes instead of one. Only damper is, it was barely warm, not served hot.

The day went by fast though. My group mostly spent the first half of the day doing roadblock procedures. A lot of us spent our downtime talking to drill sergeants, just shooting the shit really. Most of the drill sergeants talked to us now like graduates. We know they are still our leaders, but it feels like they talk to us with more respect now versus calling us little maggots. My female drill sergeant explained to us a lot of the reasons why drill sergeants are the way they are. It was mostly because we were new to this. Like a baby again because so many rules are different and it really is a separate world. They must make sure we learn what we need to learn and that we are up to speed and prepared for the next phase in our adjustment to the military. It really all does make sense. I had an idea, but my drill sergeant confirmed a lot of it and broke it down.

After we left from doing roadblock training, we had our lunch, which was an MRE, chilled out for a bit, then prepared for our next training, which was a bounding exercise. Bounding training is always fun, so I was looking forward to that. This bounding was an open field so there were a lot of blown-up cars staged, buses, civilian cut out post ups, enemy post ups, and spectators. It was pretty intense. This bounding training was the most detail-oriented we've done until this point and required the most concentration.

After training, we started packing up before going to dinner chow. We are heading back tomorrow after training so we need to be packed up by then so we can head straight out. This field training did go by fast, I must admit, and I did learn a lot while here. At the end of the day tomorrow, we will be "soldiers", at least in their eyes. The day I decided to join I considered myself a soldier. Mostly that's all a state of mind. I just didn't understand the magnitude of it. We did a lot and the time moved swiftly, so I am grateful for that.

I learned more about myself each day. Even though I don't like a lot of my battle buddies, I have learned to live with them. I have learned to work well with them. Will I keep in touch with most of them? Probably not. But they all have helped me become a better soldier. My drill sergeant says she has a nice surprise for us later (probably some damn candy), so we will see what that is. Wake up is at 04:00 so I need to finish packing. Ok, same channel, same place tomorrow. Til' then, lights out.

2/10/10

Today was great for a few reasons. First off, it didn't rain. That was definitely a plus because, the past few days, it's been rainy and cold as hell. Today was sunny and bright. It's still cold as hell, but I'll take it. We did our last basic training exercise this morning. I can't remember the name of the exercise, but it was another bounding drill, only this time, we were hopping in and out of Hum-V's covering distances. What I remember the most was how cold my hands were. I couldn't even feel my finger on the trigger of my weapon when aiming at targets. It was so cold. I could barely lock my receiver bolt to the rear for the drill instructor to inspect my weapon prior to leaving the range.

After the training drill, we had a class on I.E.D's. Improvised explosive devices. The shit you see in middle eastern war movies. Learning how to spot things out of the normal. We were trained on what to look for, which now that we have done the class, I know can pretty much be anything. They showed us things from soda cans to barrels and animal carts. After the class, we were busses back to the f.o.b. to finish packing and cleaning the training grounds. Once all the responsibilities were completed, we ate dinner chow, which was an MRE, and then proceeded for our 6-mile road march back to the main barracks.

Even though the march was 6 miles in distance, it didn't feel like a 6-mile march. Our spirits were high; we sang cadences as loud as we could. It was like we had been revived. Maybe it was an unspoken feeling of being done. The knowing that the finish line was right down the last straight and we were on that straight. We were just striding home at this point. That feeling of completion was so gratifying. If you've ever put your all into anything, played sports, or been a part of any kind of team, then you may understand the feeling. We were happy for each other and happy to have completed the task together.

CHAPTER 23
THE BONFIRE

The event that concluded the trip is what I will never forget. The bonfire ceremony. As we arrived at the barracks, I'm sure everyone on post could hear us screaming cadences from the top of our lungs. We started to approach the sand pits and we could see the glow from the flames already. The closer we got, the more excited we all got. Adrenaline was pumping, hearts were beating fast, and you could see the flames about 15 feet in the air just roaring. We came to a halt as we got to the drill pads and stared in amazement at the fire flames.

All the drill sergeants towered above us, appearing larger than life on their podium behind the fire. We all felt something grand was about to happen. All of the instructors stood with proud facial expressions as two of the senior instructors spoke about how we all have learned the army ways, and we are official soldiers now because we have successfully fulfilled all training requirements. I couldn't believe I was standing there hearing this shit. "Damn, are done." That's all I could keep thinking.

Towards the end of the speech, we were all instructed to remove our patrol caps and place atop our heads the coveted black beret. That was the best feeling I've had in a long time. To shake the drill sergeants' hands as they congratulated us on our tremendous efforts in accomplishing our first milestone on our journey to becoming elite warriors was indescribable. I wish they could've videotaped it. The entire time I thought about all the people who would be proud of me. Especially my grandparents. They were big on the military as my grandfather served in the armed forces during the Second World War. Plus, in most eyes, it is considered a respectable career.

I think I would place completing basic training on my list of major accomplishments. It's not something everyone can do. I think it's more stressful than graduating high school and maybe as stressful as taking collegiate final exams. Completing basic training requires just as much dedication and you have to be able to work well with others. The only difference is I had to do it for four years in college versus ten and a half weeks. I wouldn't trade this experience for anything.

Tomorrow starts what is called the "Recovery" phase. Recovery lasts until graduation. From this point, all we will be doing is bay maintenance, weapon cleaning, equipment turn in, and, of course, packing. Graduation is next Friday! Now that all of the phases are complete, I wonder what the reward will be. I hope we get to use our phones a bit more and get longer to eat. Tomorrow's wake up is at 07:00! To a basic training soldier, waking up at 7 a.m. is like waking up at 11 a.m. in the civilian world. I'm damn sure soaking that up. Hell, I may wake up just to go back to sleep.

It's lights out, but this time, I'm thankful for this bunk I get to lay in versus on the ground in the cold. The past few days make this bunk feel like I'm sleeping at the Hilton. I can't speak for others, but it makes me feel more appreciative for the things we don't think of that we take for granted. If I feel like this about my little bunk bed, I can only imagine how I will feel the next time I get in a real bed.

CHAPTER 24
RECOVERY/BLUE PHASE

1 /11/10

Well, today went by rather swiftly, I must say. We actually did get to sleep in until 07:00. That was freaking awesome. All we did was turn in all of our equipment and accessories for our rifles. All we really did was turn in gear and eat. We woke up, got dressed, went to breakfast chow, came back, lollygagged for a while, turned in some small stuff, then went to lunch. After lunch, we turned in all ground accessories (elbow pads, knee pads, flc vest, sleeping bags, tents, and some other things). I wanted to keep my tent and sleeping bag so bad, but they were like," Hell no"! After that was all turned in, we formed up and marched to dinner chow. One more night down and only eight left. I mailed off some pictures of me to a few friends. I feel like I look like a kid in the pictures but oh well.

We get our official A.I.T. order tomorrow. I'm hoping my training starts before March 3rd. Since I didn't get granted leave to go home, I'm hoping the sooner I can start, the sooner it can be done and then maybe I can go home for a bit. I'm not betting on it though. It may be some time before I place these feet on North Carolina soil again. Either way, I'll be leaving Fort Jackson next Saturday or Sunday. I don't have a lot to pack, but I do have a few things I'd like to send home. They told us whatever we can't pack, we must trash. We only have so many bags we are allowed to take. I'm glad I paid attention to that packing course we took. The last thing I want to do is throw something away that I just bought due to not having anything to pack it in. Okay, sleep is calling my name, plus I have guard duty tonight. Can't remember what time, but someone will wake me up to relieve them.

2/11/10

Today was pretty cool. We started our out-processing today. Leaving Fort Jackson and heading to A.I.T. I found out I was going to the Notorious Fort Knox in Kentucky. There is another guy in training with me that's going to Fort Knox as well. We have the same job (MOS) and everything. I've heard stories about Knox (as we all have), and I'm excited. I don't care that it's February and Kentucky is cold. I'm leaving here and going somewhere else I've never been. That's what's so cool to me. My journey has started. What I think makes it even better is throughout the journey, I don't know what I will see or where the Army will take me. I just know I'm gone!

We were done with out-processing by 11:00 a.m.; after that, it was "Recuperation phase." We chilled out after that and just did some weapons and equipment cleaning. We had this so-called "Surf n Turf" for lunch today but I thought it sucked. It was another mind game for starters, and on top of that, I don't eat steak. Never have, and it was barely any shrimp. To make matters worse, we were given no extra time to eat, so whoever went for the meal wasn't going to finish eating anyway. It was soldiers just trying to pile it on plates. I thought to myself, "What a waste." What was funny was when people started getting mad when drill sergeants started making them get up after the 4 minute mark. Why the fuck would they think this was different? I saw it was a set up from a mile away.

After chow, we went back to the barracks for more low-energy maintenance cleaning and recuperation. That took us back to dinner time. No one really cared what we ate today for dinner because we were all waiting for pizza and hot wings tomorrow. Granted, it was ordered from CC's Pizza which isn't the best of eateries, but hey, when you haven't had pizza in like ten weeks, it's going to be the best pizza and wings we ever had! I wouldn't have cared if it was a frozen pizza from the supermarket, I would've torn that shit up!

Moving along, you'll never guess what happened today. It fucking snowed! In the Carolinas, we hardly ever get snow and it snowed. Not only did it snow, it came down like a mini blizzard. It's probably still snowing as I write. Everyone was excited like they had never seen snow. Thinking about it now, maybe some of them haven't. Everyone was happy to the point it got annoying. Even a few drill sergeants were a little gitty. Moving forward, we got the word that wake up will be at 07:00 going forward. I have two fireguard shifts tonight but it doesn't even matter because I'm going to enjoy this sleep. I have no idea what else is on the plate for tomorrow. On a lighter note, I do know with all this snow, we won't be running tomorrow morning for p/t. It's definitely going to be ice everywhere. I bet with that being said, we will do p/t in one of the classrooms.

2/13/10

Today was relaxed. The DFAC was closed due to the snow, but that didn't stop the morning from starting off good. We ate MREs for breakfast and lunch and chilled all day. I even got to sneak in a little nap around 10:00 a.m. until noon. After lunch, I helped scrub the bay floors in preparation for our pizza party. I got stuffed at the party. Pizza, wings, brownies, cinnamon rolls, snickers. We didn't know how to act, and it wasn't a set up. We got to take our time and eat it all. We almost couldn't walk. We got so stuffed.

After dinner, we had a brigade graduation rehearsal. Today's rehearsal was making sure we all could recite the "Soldiers Creed" in unison. This sounds simple, but with over a thousand soldiers, it could take a while trying to get them to all sound like one. Foxtrot company sucks! They suck at marching, and they suck at saying the creed! Alpha company really is the best. One major thing did happen today. We got to use the phones! We were allowed 30 minutes to call whomever we wanted. Today is my sister Shakira's birthday, so I'm glad I got to talk to her today. I wish I had time to call everyone but it's cool. Word is, we will get to use the phones again on Monday.

The phone calls were the highlight of the day, that and the Dr. Pepper. I've never enjoyed a soda as much as I did today. I started collecting all contact information from those I wanted to keep in touch with. Some of the guys I have grown to know and become quite fond of. It's funny how people can grow on you. But, for better or for worse, these are my battle buddies and we are brothers and sisters. Tomorrow is the last Sunday I'll get to spend with these clowns. Friday is graduation, and by this time next week, I'll be in Kentucky starting my next chapter. So much for today, I'll consider today a victory. On to tomorrow. Lights out for now.

2/14/10

Today I did absolutely nothing. I woke up, had a great breakfast that consisted of my usual pancakes with fruit, grits, eggs, turkey sausage, strawberry yogurt, and some cereal. Not to mention, I actually got to eat it all! After breakfast, I came back to the bay to sweep and mop as I do on Sundays. I ran around somewhat frantically getting some of my battle buddies to sign my Army p/t shirt so I can frame it later on. It wasn't a boring day, just no activity. I was able to start packing my belongings in preparation for my departure for A.I.T. Some things I'll take with me but I'm sending a lot home. I told some of my battles my intention of publishing my journal entries, and they thought it was a great idea. All of them were very supportive. I let them read some of it and they loved it! Dinner chow came before we knew it, and you know after dinner chow, the day is pretty much over with. We did have a battalion formation for graduation rehearsal. It was only for an hour or so.

News flash. An interesting thing that happened today: this one chick that went AWOL and came back during Victory Forge went AWOL again today! I can't believe this chick! I mean, why come back only to go AWOL again? They called the dogs out this time. They sent out a search party, military police and all. They even had an extra formation to see if anyone knew where she was. My personal opinion is, "Fuck that bitch," let us get some sleep. Who cares about her?" Ok, well my flashlight batteries are dying. We shall continue tomorrow.

2/15/10,

Man oh man, today was very, and I do me VERY trying. I don't even know where to start. The day started off ok, like a normal day. I ate my usual breakfast, then we headed to graduation practice on the field. We all formed up and went through a dry run of the festivities. We marched to the beat of the drums and, of course, recited the soldier's creed in unison. As rehearsal continued, the clouds above released a light drizzle that just wouldn't stop. With the rain continuing, our command sergeant major excused us from the rest of the rehearsal for the day. We thought this was a good thing. Not exactly. We still had to return to the bays to clean.

The cleaning started with regular maintenance of weapons. Then, out of the blue in the middle of our cleaning rushes in another soldier from A bay screaming, "Hey, you all have to come to A bay right now, the drill sergeant is piping hot mad that someone ate her candy and doughnuts." We all looked at each other. "What the fuck that got to do with us?" Then it was explained to us that the drill sergeant left the snacks in the drill sergeant's office in bay two and someone snuck in the office and ate it all.

We all scrambled over to bay 1 to see what the hell was going on. We get there and indeed, the drill sergeant is mad as hell. Soon as we get in she is going off, " Who the hell ate all my gotdamn doughnuts and muthafuckin' Laffy fuckin Taffy?" Supposedly she bought it all for us, but the way she was mad, it seemed like she planned on keeping some for herself. About 10 seconds pass and no one says anything (like someone really was going to say they did it). "Ok, since no one wants to answer me and no one seems to know a damn thing, I'll smoke it out of you. Front leaning rest position, move," she screamed! Immediately, everyone hit the floor screaming, "Need more discipline!" we shouted. We did push-ups continuously for about 5 minutes and then she said, "I'm going give y'all one more chance to tell me, or we have gone keep going!" she shouted. I'm thinking, I don't even know what the hell is going on. No one answered again.

By this time, everyone is aggravated because no one is speaking up regarding the candy thief. The cowardly act now has us all in danger of getting disciplinary action taken against us. They even talked about not letting us graduate. On top of it all, some of these damn kids are still laughing at the situation. I almost lost my mind and whooped this one kid's ass, but then I did a good job at maintaining what's called "military bearings," and I let the shit go. Eventually (when dinner chow time came), we stopped getting smoked and resumed daily activities. My day was shot after that though.

Then there was evening graduation rehearsal. That was a complete shit show. To start, we were late arriving and in the military, you don't show up later for anything. With us being late, that meant the entire battalion was late forming up because one battalion couldn't for up without the other being properly in place. To make it worse, some platoons kept messing up on different parts of reciting the soldiers' creed so we had to recite it about 15 times before we could continue with the rehearsal. Now during rehearsal, there is no sitting down. As a matter of fact, there aren't even any chairs out on the field to sit on. It's bad enough that practice is normally about an hour and 20 minutes long standing up if everything runs smoothly. Tonight, we were out here for almost three hours. Three hours of standing in one spot. To top it off, remember all of that equipment we had to clean and turn in? Well, I had to help guard it tonight. We had to do three-hour shifts and my shift was from 23:00-02:00. It was outside, it was cold, and my hands, even though I had gloves on, felt as if I were squeezing ice cubes the entire time. I just can't wait for this to be over. The question is, can I make it without freaking killing someone's child before that? Ok, sleep is calling, and I must answer.

2/16/10

Today was okay. We had graduation practice and CC's pizza for lunch again. We didn't really do too much prior to 15:00 anyway, being that we had to wait for all of the companies to go through lunch chow. We practiced until dinner time. After dinner, we did weapons maintenance in preparation for turn in. Those weapons were filthy. We were cleaning for hours. Now, I don't mind cleaning weapons, but to have us get them to the point where they are squeaky clean is a little ridiculous. The basic training cycle that graduated before us didn't clean these weapons well for shit! But now, we have to make them look like new, that's bullshit! It's a million people that use these weapons, and they want us to make them look squeaky clean.

The day actually went by fairly quick. This morning pissed me the fuck off though. We had this bullshit battalion run with all the big wigs, sergeant majors, colonels, politicians basically. This 3-mile run had nothing to do with physical training. This was some kind of political stunt of shaking hands and shooting the shit. Old people want to still feel like they are young and a part of the fight. It's all talk. We all know if shit were to hit the fan, they would be the last to pick up a rifle. We woke up at 04:45 to prepare for this slow pace run (basically a fast walk). We were outside freezing our asses off for like a fucking hour. All this just to trot around with some old people who don't even know I personally exist. That's the kind of shit that makes me not want to go to officer school. I'm literally standing in formation thinking my hands are going to freeze and break off. My hands hurt so bad, I honestly thought about quitting. I was like, "fuck everybody this shit sucks." Then, I was able to reel my thoughts back in, gain control of my emotions, and get my head back in the game. I just had to remember, this will all be over on Friday which is in two freaking days. So, I sucked it up and completed the run.

Not a lot outside of that got on my nerves today. I did get a letter from my homeboy DJ today. He was keeping me posted on everything going on back in the "real world." Just as I thought, nothing. Same old thing still. Whenever I think about leaving, I remember DJ's letters and how there is nothing there for me to go back to that would be beneficial at this point. Tomorrow is the last day we do anything before graduation. Thursday is family day, Friday is graduation, and Saturday we leave for A.I.T. Hopefully, we will get to use the phones again. I doubt it though. If not, I don't care either way. I'll get it back on Saturday when I leave anyway. Wake up is at 06:00 tomorrow so let me get some rest. Last day, and I'm so ready to get this day over with too.

2/17/10

Today was okay at times, then there were times that I was irritated. Breakfast was great though. I got to eat everything and didn't have to rush as much as usual. From breakfast, we went to graduation rehearsal which lasted a bit longer today. We went through the entire rehearsal three times, and then we did a practice running out of the woods for family day. I'm a little worried that I won't have anyone here tomorrow for support or to spend time with. I also need to figure out how I'm going to get all this shit sent home too. My first sergeant said we can only take one duffel bag and one personal bag with us to A.I.T. Anything that doesn't fit in the bags, we had to throw out. Hopefully, someone will be here I can give something to, to take back home for me.

On a lighter note, today is the last day we have to deal with drill sergeant bullshit. Yay! Tomorrow, we will be able to go out and really venture around Fort Jackson on our own. I'm not going to jinx anything about being done, so until I'm actually on that bus headed to Kentucky, I ain't considering myself done. We will just say, I see the finish line. As far as today being productive, I got a lot done and my platoon got a lot done. We were able to get all our equipment put up from off the drill pad. That was huge because that means no more extra duties guarding the equipment. The guys in the platoon got head shaves today. That sucks because I thought for graduation haircuts we got to pick. It's cool though, not the end of the world. I also got to pack about 80% of my belongings today. I would've been able to pack everything had we not been continuously interrupted for frivolous formations. One thing I will say the Army does know how to do is waste time. Time and food. In case I haven't said it before, the army wastes tons and tons of food by not allowing soldiers to eat all their meals. It's so many people that the food could go to as far as homeless shelters, but it goes in the trash.

I believe mail has been shut down permanently shut down. It should be with only a few days left. We also had our official last dinner in the chow hall today. It wasn't anything special, it was just the last. That was all that happened today. I have fireguard duty at 2 a.m. Fireguard doesn't end until Friday night. Hopefully, there will be a lot of things to say about tomorrow.

CHAPTER 25
GRADUATION

2/18/10

Today was family day and it was AMAZING! We woke up at 05:00 and went to chow, then got all packed up. I brought all my things down to the drill pad to load on the 1-ton truck to take to graduation for my family to put in their car. We cleaned up the bays a little bit, then marched down to the field for the ceremonies. Once we got there, I could see all the stands filled with people waiting in anticipation for graduation. We couldn't really see what was going on on the field. We were behind the field in the woods, crouched down waiting to run out to greet our families. I could hear the drums here and there. I would occasionally be able to make out bits and pieces of some of the speeches that were given by some of the base leaders and officers. After a while, I realized that the ceremonies were more so for the family members than for us. I didn't care though. As long as they enjoyed it, all I cared about was being done with basic training and going somewhere to get a good meal.

Once we ran out on the field, the crowd roared with excitement. Family members, friends, and other soldiers and base staff cheered. The band played, balloons blew and flew around. It was a site to see, I'll admit. Everyone screamed so loud, you would think we were superstars walking around. The family members saw this as a glorious milestone, while we were just happy to go eat. I didn't expect anyone to show up for me, so I teamed up with a battle buddy and we set out to explore the huge base. It was people everywhere and anywhere there was to go on base. I bet all these small businesses on base make a fortune off these graduation events. Parents and soldiers were buying up any and everything that said "Army" on it. I mean, I saw people buying bullshit like erase holders that had army logos on them. What the hell? The hottest seller item I think I saw was T-shirts. "Proud mom, dad, sister, brother, cousin, uncle, grandparent"- you name it. They had a T-shirt. It was soldiers who spent their entire three months' worth of savings in the post exchange store. What's funny is, most of this shit people buying, you can't even take to A.I.T. A lot of that stuff you have to earn as a privilege at the next level.

As for me, I want to get settled into my new living quarters and a new way of life before I get concerned with buying all this bull-shit. Nevertheless, the soldiers and parents bought it all up and the stores made a killing off of them. As the day progressed, I ate and ate and ate whenever I felt like it or saw something I hadn't had in 3 months. The main thing I craved that I didn't realize, was the ice-cream. I think I had like three or four milkshakes today, all strawberry cheesecake from Sonic. I ate a lot of food too, but it was the milkshakes my heart desired. About 5:30 or 6:00 p.m. I made up my mind I wanted to get back to the drill pad and the barracks a little early to rule out any possibility of being late for evening formation.

I decided to get one last bite to eat and head back. As I was sitting down to enjoy my last meal at Fort Jackson, one of my battle buddies yelled out, "Tucker!" I looked up and was filled with joy to see none other than my sister and my stepdad. Imme-diately, I rushed to them, forgetting all about my food. I can't tell you how happy I was to see them. I wasn't expecting to see anyone until tomorrow. There they were, right in front of me. As I ate, I sat and listened to them explain to me how long they had been looking for me and how many dummy missions they had gone on. I spent the last two free hours with them going around post until it was time to report back to formation. I tried to describe to them where I would be in the formation tomorrow, so they could look for me as we marched in and out. I said my goodbyes and exited the rental vehicle on my way to formation.

No sooner had I turned the corner than I saw none other than my friend Monica! I was like, holy shit! I didn't expect to see her until tomorrow. That really completed my day! I was beside myself. I was so excited. Seeing everyone emotionally was very fulfilling. I mean, just think, she drove all the way down here from Charlotte to Columbia, which is about an hour-plus drive after getting off of work. How awesome is that? Knowing she would only get to see me for a few moments. I don't know a lot of people that would do that. I gave her a huge hug, explained to her I didn't have much time to talk, and walked with her back to her car. I hugged her once again and told her I would see her in the morning at the ceremonies.

I went to formation completely satisfied with the day. I couldn't have asked for anything else from today. I will sleep well tonight. Tomorrow will be even better! Not only do I get to see everyone, but tomorrow we get to leave post. We couldn't leave today; we just got to explore everything without having to run or march everywhere. I don't know why but for some reason, I concluded I wanted to eat at Chili's tomorrow. Chili's isn't even my favorite restaurant, nor do I even have a favorite meal from there. But, that's what I have a taste for, so damn it, that's where I'm going. Tomorrow may be the last day I see loved ones again until possibly summer, sometime around July. I know a lot of them still have questions that haven't been answered when it comes to why I left and why I enlisted in the service. I'm sure once they see me walk across that stage they will understand why. Well, lights out. Truly excited for tomorrow, I am.

2/19/10

Today was graduation day! Everything was great, I must say. My sister, stepfather, and all my closest female friends came to support me. I can't even name everyone because some friends brought other friends too. I was ecstatic! The ceremony wasn't too long. The weather was sunny and bright. Everything went according to plan. How often does that happen? After the graduation ceremony, we did go to eat. We didn't go to Chili's. We went to Golden Corral instead. Everyone else agreed on that choice and I was cool with it. I really didn't care. I got stuffed anyway. After we ate, everyone wanted to go back to the post exchange to shop and buy things. I don't know why civilians are so fascinated with the post exchange shop. That's all they talked about and that's all they all wanted to do.

Once we left the store, my sister and stepfather departed back for Charlotte. I was slightly disappointed, but I understood they were tired. I was satisfied with seeing them and them being here to support me. It just felt rushed for some reason. I hate feeling rushed. I don't feel like they rushed me. It just felt like there wasn't enough time in the day. Joy and Shakira left because they needed to get back to work, and I felt like I was holding everyone else hostage. They assured me I wasn't, and they were enjoying themselves. So, I thought no more of it and continued to enjoy my time with them.

Now, the one thing I wanted to do that I said I was going to do while I was out for the day was get a tattoo. We were not supposed to get tattooed, and I knew it. I didn't give a shit. It was my last day. If this had been the winter break, no, I wouldn't have done it, but I knew I was leaving tomorrow and the chances of anyone seeing it were minimal. Monica thought I was crazy for doing it. I was on the fence about it because I knew it would take away from us spending time together. I didn't want them just sitting there for hours while I got tatted up. They were fine with going. I knew we were running out of time and if I was going to do it we needed to go now. So we went and luckily, I made it back to post just in time with about 20 minutes to spare prior to formation.

I hate feeling like I'm running out of time. I rushed out of Monica's car so fast, I left my wallet. She had to turn around to bring it back to me. Not to mention I left my coat in my sister's car! Now I'm coatless, headed to Kentucky in the wintertime. Not a good way to start A.I.T. Great day, horrible ending! I had no one else to be mad at either because it was my fault. I didn't get to say goodbye to a lot of people, but that's okay. When they get their copies of this book, they will get their goodbyes.

Basic training is over! Man, what a thrill, what a blast! I can't even put it all in words. But I tried. At times it felt like the longest journey in the world. Today is not one of those days. Today made the past few months seem like moments. The funny thing is, at this very moment, I'm glad I went through every bit of it. I can even say there are some points. Looking back, I'm thinking, the drill sergeants should've smoked us for the things we did and we probably got off the hook for more things than I realized. They were more like parents now that I reflect on it. It was tough love, that's what it was. As I look at their faces now, I see pride, I see relief, I see happiness. Now I understand why they chose to do what they do. That must feel great seeing your babies graduate.

This has been a tremendous experience for me and I'm sure it's been the same for my battle buddies. Everyone's proud of me and has expressed that feeling. I feel as if I'm off to a good start finally toward something beautiful in my life. It's not about the Army, just a change for the better in general in my life. I have pushed myself further physically, mentally, and emotionally than I ever have in my life. It was always easy as a ki or in a child-like mind-state to find an excuse or reason for why something wouldn't or couldn't get done. Now I know for a fact I can do way more than the limits I place on myself. You, as the reader, can do more than the limitations you place on yourself.

I have realized that life isn't about what others think of you. It's not about all of the items you can purchase. It's about feelings, controlling emotions, and steering thought to achieve outcomes that better yourself. It's about grasping the moment, really embracing life, and using challenges as learning opportunities. Greatness can be achieved for everyone. Greatness is what you want it to be for you. Greatness is seeing and working harder towards your personal goals and being in tune with your inner emotions. I think basic training has freed me of a fear-based mentality and has taught me to think calmly in stressful situations, to realize there are alternative ways to solving problems. I've grown in more ways than I ever thought I would. I have a feeling this won't be the last of my documentation, and this certainly won't be the last of my journeys. This is the beginning. I just hope you stay tuned.

ACKNOWLEDGMENTS

I first and foremost, would like to thank God for creating me and allowing me to grow, blossom, and mature in ways that allow me to learn and spread love. God has shown me beauty in struggle and pain. I thank the highest for keeping me in a good head space to complete this document. I know through His love I am able to do all things possible. To my mother, Cassandra, you departed from this life way too soon, yet I am still learning from you decades later. Your determination lives in me. To my grandparents, you were the epitome of a foundation and the root of our family. I learned commitment and focus through you. I learned how to weather the storm because of you. I learned how to love because of you. To everyone in my personal life that has made me who I am today. I thank my friends for allowing me to see their struggles to learn from and grow from. I was always the youngest in my crew growing up, and my friends and I are more like brothers, so to them, I thank them. Cedric, Barry, Kyle, Jason my achievements are your achievements. You guys have inspired me to do things my way because each of you has always done things your way, and I respect the hell out of that. I have learned through you guys that determination can't be waivered. If you make a decision and stick with it. To my friend and brother Morris, I appreciate you challenging me creatively and putting the fire under me to complete this journey by completing your journey. You made me realize this dream isn't dead, and it was you who gave me the last push unknowingly to finish this document. To Joy, Shakira, Janiya, and Kesha, I thank you for being my true "family." There's a difference between family and relatives, and you guys are most certainly family. We cry together, laugh together, and will succeed together. To Monica, I thank you for believing in me and all my talents. You will all always be appreciated. To DJ, my friend and my brother, you have always been supportive and believed in me, but mostly you helped me believe in myself. To my wife Sheridan and my kids Jason, Marielle, and Mariyah, I thank you for challenging me and being my place of refuge. I will always love you guys; I will always cherish you guys, and I hope you know I live to love you! To all those I haven't mentioned by name, please know that your presence, support, guidance, and love have not gone unnoticed. Each one of you has played an intricate part in my journey and has left an indelible mark on my heart. I am eternally grateful for every lesson, every smile, every challenge, and every moment shared. Thank you for being a part of my story.